ONE HELL OF A TOOTHACHE

A CANCER SURVIVOR'S TALE

ROBERT APPLE PIOMBINO

Copyright © 2018 Robert Apple Piombino
All rights reserved
First Edition

PAGE PUBLISHING, INC.
New York, NY

First originally published by Page Publishing, Inc. 2018

ISBN 978-1-64298-040-0 (Paperback)
ISBN 978-1-64298-041-7 (Digital)

Printed in the United States of America

For Corina

DARK MATTER

A DREAM STRIPPED OF ITS CONTENTS AS THE DAWN,
CRASHES THRU THE NIGHT SKY, TRANSCENDING REALITY.
CREATING ITS OWN FLAWED MEMORY, THOUGHTS ARE REBORN
AGAINST THE BACKDROP OF NOW, AND MOLDED
THROUGH OUR INDIVIDUAL PRISMS, AND DASHED AGAINST
THE STONE CROPPED BORDERS OF OUR OWN CHOOSING.

WE AWAKEN EACH DAY TO A NEW BEGINNING, OBLIVIOUS TO OUR
FRAILTIES, SHAPED BY THE MORALS OF THE DAY, WEATHERED
BY OUR OWN FAILINGS. WE TROD THROUGH THE UPS AND DOWNS
OF OUR INDIVIDUAL WORLDS. ALONGSIDE OTHERS BUT MOSTLY
KEEPING TO OURSELVES. WE SPEND OUR LIMITED TIME
IN BATTLE AFTER BATTLE WITHOUT THERE EVER BEING A VICTOR.

INTO THIS BACKGROUND WE ENDURE PAIN AFTER PAIN
DISAPPOINTMENT AFTER DISAPPOINTMENT
WISHING FOR THE GOOD TO OUTLAST AND OUTWEIGH THE BAD.
ACCEPTING THIS BLEAK REALITY, EVEN A GLIMMER OF LIGHT
OF HOPE BECOMES A BEACON
TO GUIDE US AND COMFORT OUR MORTAL PRESENCE.

LIFE AFTER ALL IS NEVER IMAGINED AS A PERMANENT PLACEMENT
BUT IS REDUCED TO BEING JUST THE TIME BEFORE DEATH WHERE
SOMETIMES ANGELS BRING US HOPE AND DEVILISH IMPS
WHISPER EVIL INTO OUR TINY BRAINS AND HEARTS.
WE CHOOSE OUR COURSE, AND SOME CHOOSE TO LIVE
A RIGHTEOUS EXISTENCE, AND OTHERS SIMPLY WALLOW IN FILTH.

Depriving others and feasting on the suffering of others
pestilence, a scourge ravishing the flesh,
the Dark Prince of all maladies, again, joins life's struggle.
The mind holds strong to the very end.
I chose not an entry into the fray
nor did I choose the means to leave it.

But the donnybrook has begun
mortally weakened by the parting of my matriarch.
I ask God to let her progeny fight against
the forces that seek only to end that which was
and allow the simple means to an end
not chosen but given fully.

To now enter without my life's companion
is to enter the darkness without conception
or knowledge of past or future
since none exist in this barren wilderness
where light and love are strangers.
I desire only a swiftness to the final demise.

A vision of hope eludes my conscience
as I wander through and into the vast unknown.
The wonders of past times and events
stream by in a cavalcade of dull colors
permeating the solidness of my prison,
leaving not odor nor sound.

'Tis folly to seek my destiny without regard
to that which I am without or have lost.
Nay I will not an inch forward proceed
nor a moment pass until time immemorial
and another heaven and earth pass
only then my soul shall rest.

To soar amongst a heavenly sky
and become laden with riches galore
is no temptress or taunting to none but the foolhardy
for love, and only love can bear such gifts
that dreamers and poets and lovers
share and give and receive without regret.

For Corina
3.15.15 rap

PROLOGUE

My journey began in June 2008 when the ER doctor ran in to tell me he found a tumor, a cancer in my kidney, which had to be removed, and then he ran right back out, never to hear my questions and never any effort to ease the shock left in his wake. I was so helpless and scared, unable to express my feelings to others, unable to believe what had happened to me, thinking I was alone, battling the indescribable emotions that had taken over my mind, searching for answers, asking, "Why me?" rejecting the reality of the moment. I was nearly knocked out emotionally and physically when out of the blue he said I had cancer and my kidney had to be removed. This body of mine that I thought was under my control, by my mind and my will, had suddenly and viciously attacked itself, and without any warning it was now going to be cut, and pieces of me were going to be removed. How horrible, how truly gruesome suddenly my life had become. A whole ugly new world was opening up to swallow me pieces at a time.

My body was no longer mine, and my mind was quickly heading down the same path. In a matter of minutes, I was thrown into this new world, where no friends, no family, and no happiness was allowed to go. Tears and mind games were my faithful companions. Death, a former stranger to this once youthful, fun-filled man, had suddenly become a viable alternative. A not-so-ugly face had been shown to me, and in my helpless and desperate condition, embracing this former nemesis seemed like an oh-so-easy thing to do. Wicked in my thoughts of any future happiness, and with wanton disregard for reality or alternative paths to travel, I allowed myself to be engulfed by all the fears and horror that had accumulated over a lifetime. Every horrible thing I saw, heard, or was told about cancer was rushing to my brain. My life was basically over, but I was still sucking in air, and walking and still capable of thoughts, just horrible thoughts. Maybe it was a mistake, I would awake, and it was just a miserable, horrid, decrepit nightmare, and I can get back to my "normal" existence. But what was my normal existence? It surely wasn't that concerned with others and their conditions. In fact, I was hardly ever aware of my own. Rarely had I visited a doctor, or read an ingredients label, or even thought about cancer. My so-called lifestyle would actually improve by my being more concerned with all aspects of life and a realization of the burdens so many of us have to bear in our lives, and unless you asked, most people struggle by in silence. This would not be me.

I announced to anyone that listened about my cancer and only having one kidney. After four years of survival, people who have cancer in their lives usually talk to me first about it because of my being so vocal and open on the subject. I suppose this is how I cope with the cancer and how I have tried very hard to make cancer easy to talk about and treat it like any other disease, something to fight and deal with, along with help from friends and the community. I meet many people at the kidney walks and the Susan G. Komen for the cure walks in the park. I stand side by side with my fellow sister warriors and feel proud that we're doing something and helping others.

I eventually had the operation, a radical hand-assisted (due to the tumor's large size) laparoscopic nephrectomy, and recovered, and felt sorry for myself, but was finally able to rationalize my thoughts, and figure out I was a whole lot luckier than other folks. I was able to start trying to research this RCC (Renal Cell Carcinoma) and see what could be done to help myself. Discovering how different kidney cancer was compared to most others, I came across something on the Internet about or from Steve Dunn (an author of several books on kidney cancer). Then I read everything available but saw that there were still not a lot of options for me. There was adjuvant care, and I wanted to know more about metastatic cancer and how it spreads. I was somewhat dismayed at the realization, being told by the doctor we got it all, and that he was not recommending any chemo or radiation treatments, that this was not an altogether true and accurate diagnosis and prognosis of my condition. Not being well versed or experts in RCC, their prognosis is limited in accuracy, and any proposed treatment would have little or no effect on my condition. I was just supposed to wait and get CT scans to find the dreadnought if it appeared and metastasized. Without knowing, I had become a warrior and seeker of knowledge. I was going to discard any of the clichés I was being told, I was going to learn all I could, and I was going to live, not continue to die, by self-pity. I had become immune to talk of things that can't be done. Now diet and what I put into my body have become paramount. Anything I could discover about how cancer grows and spreads was my daily lesson. Knowledge is power, and I wanted all the power I could get, so when and if this dread cancer returns, I can be prepared to fight, and indeed I will fight.

I have cried and laughed, and I have grown and become strong and a lot less fearful of where my life is going and what I could do to help keep myself healthy. I greet each day with a wonder that only a child has, an innocence and acceptance of anything that can happen. The sign above my entranceway door states "Every day is a gift." Every time I leave the house and look at those words, I realize how true it is to be alive this day, and I can do with it the best I can and celebrate the simple fact that I am alive. There is no way I would ever say I was glad that I have cancer, but I will forever say that my life has been made better. I laugh and am happy more completely, and I appreciate life more in myriad ways since the vile cell growth was made known to me. I believe my life has improved, and I have become more human, more compassionate, and more aware of how we as a species do remarkable things and endure such intolerable circumstances because life is so very precious. I find some simple joy and pleasure every day, sunrises or sunsets, children playing, flowers blooming, birds chirping, random acts of kindness either witnessed or done by oneself. Just being alive is like my sign above the door, a gift, a wonderful gift, and one that can be shared or enjoyed alone.

Cancer is not concerned with race, creed, religious beliefs or if you've been good or bad at any time in your life. Sinners and saints are both fodder for a cancer to establish itself. I would tell them your life will never be the same, and everything you do, you will balance and base your decision according to your cancer, whether it's NED (No Evidence of Disease) or not. It will never leave your thoughts or your conscience. It makes you more aware of ingredients in your food purchases, more concerned with household cleaning products, and more concerned with anything you come in contact with. The darkest cloud having a silver lining is a metaphor not that inappropriate for cancer survivors. I recall a friend of mine while shopping was having trouble deciding whether or not to buy a certain toothpaste. I asked him what was the dilemma over toothpaste, and he replied that it was buy the two tubes and get two more free. He said he didn't know if he would be around long enough to use them. We laughed, and I took advantage of the sale price as well. He was stage IV with mets in his lung, and this event happened before I was found with my cancer. We still talk about it today.

I recall while in the hospital, I was becoming aware of how so many of life's functions go on without anyone having to be aware of them or to even have to think of them. I had just spent the better part of the day concentrating on my digestive system, trying to actually control it with my conscious thoughts and trying to bring about by sheer willpower that which occurs naturally without even a thought given to its successful completion. I was becoming more aware of self and starting to have appreciation of all that we take for granted every day and every moment we live. How much clearer things now appeared! So much awareness of life was now made known to this temporarily bedridden soul. It was like an awakening had occurred. I started to think that how incredible this cancer was, that an errant mutation of a cell was so darn determined to live that against all the odds, against all the safeguards that are in our bodies to defend against such an onslaught, that it was able to survive in a world that was dead set against its survival.

My immune system had failed and allowed this cell to become a dominant part of me. Yet I still thought that even this cancer cell was actually a part of me, so how could the immune system recognize it as an enemy and attack it? For as bad as the terrible child is, he is still our child and our flesh and blood, so we don't kill our defective offspring but attempt to correct and control, which is how I was starting to look at my own cancer cells. My own body was trying to destroy my own body. The concept was fascinating, and this cancer cell had not just survived but had thrived and multiplied to the state where it had now taken over my kidney, and if nothing was done, it would certainly have taken over the host body, which would be me.

I thought that even this successful compromising of my normal cells with the cancer cells was truly amazing; that the end result would eliminate any chance for the cancerous continuation of life, so any success is doomed for failure, for if the cancer were to succeed, it would kill me. What a complicated and absorbing flood of thoughts had taken over my mind. A brief few weeks ago, I had given little thought to cancer. My thoughts were of the price of a gallon of milk or a gallon of gas, and now cancer was the sole object of my scrutiny and conscious thoughts. I was a prisoner in my own body to this disease, and if I let it, I would be a prisoner in spirit as well. I felt in a way that cells from my body, even mutated cancer oncogenes, were a part of me, and how ironic that parts of me were on a mission of survival, which would inevitably become a death mission. My own death squad was out to destroy me by fighting for their survival, not mine. I couldn't think of any kind of symbiotic relationship, that both parties are destroyed at the end. This was truly a complicated revelation that I rolled around inside me for quite some time. We dismiss thoughts and ideas, bad thoughts and dark imaginings removed easily, and wonderful pleasing thoughts regretfully fall as well. Memories fade and dreams subside. Goals, once so attainable, fall from reach. The time we're given seems never enough. Time that lingers, perhaps providing reason, and time that flees, taking with it a cure. The child we were is no longer here. The little baby has grown and shed its features, replaced over and over by newer versions of ourselves until replication ceases to function, and the telomeres on our cells no longer permit cellular replacement. Eventually I figured out that there are so many pieces of ourselves that we render useless and discard, that it was okay to think of the cancer cells as enemies, out to hurt us. I thought about infections we get, where great amounts of mucous and puss are produced, yet we don't harbor any attachments or worry that it's a part of us. I thought about waste removal on a

13

cellular level, cell regeneration, and all the pieces of our bodies that are constantly being replicated and replaced daily, resulting in almost a whole body being replicated, repeatedly throughout our lifetime.

Incessantly we are disposing of pieces of our very existence. Knowingly or not, the process continues till the body stops the balancing act, when homeostasis and respiration, can no longer produce desirable results. Death on a cellular plane, apoptosis, is pre-programmed and designed to eradicate the genetic mutations from conquering the normal replication process, yet this too can falter and allow cancer to multiply with impunity.

I realized life itself was the gift I had long ignored and that even now I was receiving such amazing gifts. My incidental finding of my cancer during a botched biopsy, without which I probably would have died by now, is a gift I enjoy daily. I doubt much that the gift of life itself was ever more appreciated than by someone who was snatched back from death's door, or who was given a medical death sentence but still wakes each day to sunrises, smiles, and perhaps a fresh cup of coffee.

Whenever somebody relates some self-perceived terrible incident in their lives, something that happened on the way to work, like they missed the bus, had a flat tire, or got pulled over for a traffic ticket, I listen for the point when after all the complaining, they say something like "you wouldn't believe it" or "how annoying it was." I marvel at what some people find a bad experience, and then I agree with them and add to the dialogue about how wrong it was to leave the lid up on the toilet, the lid off on the ketchup, and wished they'd put a lid on themselves. I sometimes race my wife to the corner, and sometimes I'll win and sometimes I lose, but either way we laugh at the two of us with canes hobbling down the street and people standing around can't figure out what we're doing—why is he chasing her or she chasing him? When I park in a handicap spot, I always say out loud, "Damn this cancer has paid off again."

I walked into my oncologist's waiting room with my brother, also a cancer survivor, for the first time, and said to all the people in the NYC office, "Hi, I guess you all got cancer or you'd be somewhere else," "anywhere else," "We're from Jersey," and "We have cancer too." "Okay, you can all go back to staring at the walls now." "Boy this is sure one tough crowd." "Anybody here know any good cancer jokes?" It seemed to me that the best way to conquer fear is with some other emotion; any other emotion will suffice, and for me attempts at humor, whether humorous or not, do the trick and chase the fear from many topics and life situations. Thus my entrance into most doctors' offices brings about an outpouring of emotions followed by an unusual degree of concern from most patients and all medical personnel.

So I guess that's how I cope, compensate, overcome, enjoy, and rejoice, mainly because with few exceptions my life is normal. I use the word *normal* because I don't know a more accurate or precise word to use. *Normal* has a connotation to it that is not what I mean by the word, because there are so many meanings that don't fit, but just about *normal* is the best word to use for the time being.

I believe the ability to rejoice is the most significant trait to maintain the fact that we are alive and get to see our loved ones grow and prosper. We rejoice in our regained ability to engage in activity or even just to watch someone else doing something, like a baseball or football game. Those would be the most common I would guess if you were to compile some type of list that we could all fill out and send in. I, on the other hand, have some things that may seem odd or not as important to most people I guess. I rejoice each and every time I urinate, I think of how my one surviving kidney is filtering the blood, removing salts and chemicals, and adding what I need to survive. I rejoice that the kidney does this, the filtering, the maintaining of homeostasis, keeping blood pressure at certain levels, and making urine that is eliminated from the body. It does this daily without any input from me and regardless if I am aware of what it does or not. I rejoice in being alive, being able to walk in the park and smell the flowers in bloom. I enjoy the snow falling on my face, and I rejoice at my having survived and lived to be able to do all those things that one considers normal. But most of all, I rejoice at being able to love my wife and my family, and to enjoy life wherever it takes me during my time on this planet.

With absolutely the greatest respect for the caregivers, who are certainly heaven's angels temporarily assigned to earthly duties, I add the following words without any disrespect or egotism. Unless one is subjected to the actual things that are done to cancer patients including organ removal and the gut-wrenching fears accompanying such barbaric procedures, unless the words "you got cancer" reverberate in your mind like echoes of the canyon walls, until the actual realization that your own body has let you down and is poised to kill you, until you have gone through denial, fear, and eventual acceptance, you cannot know the true conditions of what we go through. Just what we allow to escape our minds, the words we use to describe pain and frustration, are not ever understood by anyone that hasn't been there. The frustrations are never really gone, but we make them appear to be for the sake of the person taking care of us. Never wanting to be a burden, when all you are is a burden, is such a lonely and unfamiliar place to all except those that reside there. Truly blessed are the caregivers, without whom our experiences with this evil malady would certainly be intolerable. To the caregivers this book is dedicated.

CHAPTER 1

THE BEAST THAT NEVER EVEN ROARED

Once upon a time about several years ago I was suffering from a very bad toothache. I didn't like going to the dentist but finally got up the courage to go to one. So I called up, made an appointment, and felt proud of myself that I was going to overcome my fears and was going to get relief from all this pain.

The dentist gave me a prescription for an antibiotic, and he insisted that I get it filled, and he told me to start taking it right away. Following his advice, I took the medicine and got sick, very sick, and sick to my stomach. Sick so bad that no food stayed in me longer than a minute before I had to rush to the bathroom. Everything whether eaten or drunk came rushing out of me. I was unable to even keep soup or broth in me. All the so-called "good" bacteria in my digestive tract had died from the powerful antibiotics prescribed by my dentist for my hell of a toothache. It took weeks to get my digestive system back to normal by eating my least favorite food— yogurt. I ate the stuff because it was the only food that didn't come back out right away, and it was filled with beneficial bacteria needed in the gut.

So there I was, sick as a dog, about as sick as you can be and not be confined to a bed, forcing myself to go to work, believing that I could somehow make it through a night by not eating. At least the toothache was gone. So to work I went. When I get there, my boss tells me that I'm not allowed in the building, or on site, because I haven't been able to get my pass yet from the Port Authority of NY and NJ. He stated that I wouldn't be allowed on airport property without this pass, so go home and don't worry. Amazing how people always seem to tell you not to worry, right after they give you something to worry about—a yin-yang thing, I guess, a balance of good and evil, perhaps more likely a good time to start worrying.

Feeling sick inside from the bad reaction to the medicine, and sick about not being allowed in the building, I figured a more sinister reason was responsible for this edict from the boss, who was waiting for me outside my job. He acted like nothing was wrong and he would allow me in when the pass was issued by the PA. After my repeated requests for some further explanation, he again advised me not to worry and that my pay wouldn't be affected by my not being on the job. Continuing to ask for a more valid reason for this unexpected event, he added more intrigue to his original excuse about not having proper ID, stating untruths that were provably false. He claimed they spotted me on the airport property without a pass, which was false. I asked to meet my accuser but was told to go home and don't worry about it. Well, this went on for close to two weeks, and my actions the very next day after not being allowed in the building were almost prophetic, as will be revealed in the ensuing pages, without prejudice or too much embellishment, excepting of course where the overwhelming blandness demands spicing.

I decided to take the opportunity of being "off" work to go to the doctor. I figured, what could go wrong? My insides had all been cleared out by the powerful antibiotics, and there was no job to go to, so what better time to see about going on disability, after all I wasn't allowed in the building, had herniated disks in my back, and was feeling really lousy. Later on when me and my wife called to tell the boss I had gone to the hospital, the boss told me he fired me two weeks ago on Tuesday. I replied I was on disability since the Monday before that Tuesday.

He said, "I'll just backdate it then."

Can you imagine someone saying something like this? I couldn't understand the reason for all the hostility, but was glad I went on disability. I never could believe that a company could fire you when you were on disability, but it was definitely true, and my cost to keep the insurance had increased astronomically, and I even had to pay nearly a thousand dollars for a few days' continuance of my coverage or let it expire. What a week it was.

My visit to the doctor revealed more health issues than I could have ever predicted. He suggested to get a biopsy of my liver because it appeared fatty on some previous test. I didn't recall if it was a blood test that revealed this or the MRI that showed three herniated disks at L3, L4, and L5. In any case, the die was cast, and I would soon to be engulfed by the medical world, with all the modern techno innovations and latest devices to pierce, poke, dissect, inject, and inspect every nook and cranny of my body. I would also be lucky enough to meet the most professional dedicated purveyors of care, yet unfortunate enough to meet the dregs of the medicinal under-body of medicine, where bare-bone pseudo-medical practitioners toil away at making even the simplest task an overwhelming ordeal. Both persuasions can be found in the following pages and in your local medical establishment, hopefully more of the former than the latter of the two.

A week or so prior to these events, I went to a back pain special-ist, a neurologist who suggested I get an epidural, which he said he could do right there in his office. I was just supposed to lift up my shirt and bend over the desk while he plunged a hypodermic needle into my lower spine and injected some drug. Can you imagine being told something like this? This crazy idea never materialized because the doctor had a friend of his visiting him in the office that day, a sur-geon from the hospital down the street. He suggested after hearing me questioning the sanity of such a procedure that he could make an appointment for me to have the epidural done at the hospital, with complete anesthesia. My acceptance was immediate.

I had never had or even heard of an epidural, so I was somewhat nervous, as any procedure requiring you to be placed unconscious has its danger, and it was, after all, a surgical procedure. The epidural was done at the hospital. I was completely anesthetized, no complica-tions, and the back pain I had suffered for years, decades, was nearly gone. Miraculous, I thought, what was in that epidural, and does it last forever? Silly questions, but I felt great right away after awakening from the anesthesia.

So when my doctor suggested the need to get a liver biopsy, and I wasn't allowed to go to work, I no longer had a job, and my medical benefits would be canceled, I agreed to get it done. I said OK. I had a bad experience with the antibiotics, but the epidural was a hospital procedure, and it went well. Plus, I assumed the biopsy would be no worse or more complicated than the epidural. So I was now going for my second trip to the hospital in the same month, which happened to be December. Merry Christmas.

After an endless wait on an undersized hospital gurney, dressed in the standard open-back and patient-frustrating hospital garb, I was finally wheeled into an elevator. Then down a hall, bounced off walls and uneven floors where I found myself in a small room that was separated into even smaller cubicles by track-mounted curtains. From my vantage point, I could only see the dirty stained ceiling tiles, wondering if some substance leaked from above or some human fluid had splashed upward from this labyrinth from hell. I passed the time listening to the heated exchanges between what I assumed were the doctor and the nurses. Perhaps they were discussing what treatments or procedures were being done to the other victims in the room, or which sauce they liked best on their pita bread. Like being in a third world country, I couldn't even make out what language was being spoken, whether it was Hindu or Arabic, but it wasn't anything I could make any sense out of, or determine if it was good or bad. At least I wasn't having a spinal tap, where they stick a needle in your spine.

Several years ago, suffering from severe back pain, on disability, and willing to do anything to find out the cause of all the pain, I allowed myself to be given this procedure. I was told to lie down on this cold stainless steel table. They tilted the table several degrees with my head higher than my feet and told me not to move or you could lose the ability to walk or worse. Yet the more they tilted the table, the more I started to slide off, so the tighter I gripped to the underside to maintain my position.

The scene must have seemed odd to the uninitiated as I was naked on my stomach with some semblance of a gown not covering my backside with doctors and nurses musing about as if the world was fine and everything was normal.

When they began to wipe down my back with some substance they repeated the mantra. "Don't move." As I was sliding off the end of the freezing cold table, the doctor inserted a large syringe into my back. His target was the void between the spinal cord and the spinal column, a severely critical mark, one not easily tolerable of mistakes. His goal was to remove some undisclosed measure of spinal fluid. As he inserted the needle, which I clearly felt, I was slowly falling more and more off the end of the table. The good doctor at this crucial point in time was jokingly recalling his last golf outing with the other good doctors and telling the nurse next to me his golf score. Slowly he started to retract the plunger and remove my precious bodily fluids as steadily I continued my gravitational slide toward the hospital operating room floor.

The whole time I was thinking what parts of my body would and would not function normally after this sojourn into the soft underbelly of the medical world and its arcane rituals and antiquated practices. I don't recall any results of this test, besides my decision to not ever take up golf. I never heard anything one way or the other about it, and because it was such a horrible experience, I render it to the junkyard in my mind of things best not to think about.

Back to my tale …

After convincing myself to stay in this spot and not get too excited over the less than inspiring surroundings I found myself in, I was determined to see this procedure through to the end, and any thought I had of getting up and coming back another day were summarily dismissed, as I was not going through this again, so I lay there staring at the decaying ceiling and hoped for the best.

At last the doctor and nurse came bursting into my little world, and without any greeting or explanation of the coming events, they told me to roll over on my side. Then some cold jellylike substance was spread on me like grape jelly on toast. It was cold and felt a little silly, but I quickly switched from simple discomfort to complete awareness and solid alertness when he said, "OK, I'm going to stick a needle in you." "OK," I said, "what about a local anesthetic to ease the pain, and then come back in a little while after it gets numb?"

I must have jumped off the table when he sent that needle into my body, quick without any time to plead for anything. It was jabbed into me. I don't know how many of them were holding me down and telling me to be still, but I figured the hard part was over, so I said, "OK, let's get it done." I heard some crackling sounds, a clicking noise from the tool they had inside me to snip off tiny little pieces of my liver. I heard a lot of this sound, but I didn't know what it was till weeks later.

Then the doctor informs me that he's going in deeper, so remain still. Deeper, are you kidding me, it feels like you're already into my spinal cord, how much deeper are you going? I'm now screaming in pain, and saying all types of curses, and profanity. Then deeper it goes, and I'm in the worst pain I ever felt. I thought the needle had penetrated my brain, screaming with several people holding me down. They mercifully said they were done, and the smiling-faced doctor said, "See it wasn't all that bad." I swore to myself I would catch up to this guy in the parking lot someday and beat the crap out of him. That was all I could think off, revenge against this beast of a doctor, with piss-poor skills, no bedside manner, and an overzealous desire to inflict pain and enjoy the aftermath.

On a scale of 1 to 10, the pain tearing through me was about 110. What a thing to put yourself through. I mean it's not like I got shot or something, it was voluntary, and I wasn't in any danger that required I get this done. It was just a simple suggestion. It was just a simple medical procedure that only required a local injection and a simple insertion of a needle to remove a tiny little piece of my liver. I was told there might be some minor discomfort. The pain caused by this procedure I have so deeply embedded in my being that I can't even allow myself to remember the depth of it. I intentionally and successfully have repressed it into the places in my brain that even I dare to tread—a total elimination, a safety measure, to ensure sanity for the remainder of my mortal existence on this planet.

I was covered with a blanket, and then bounced once again, over the uneven floors, each bump inflicting even more pain. I was "parked" in the hallway. I couldn't get up, or sit up, and I was calling out for help. There were other gurneys and patients lined in the hallways, some moaning, and some may be in too much pain to even produce a sound. I lay there unattended for about an hour. My wife happened by this hall and heard me and got a nurse to come to my aid with some morphine. Yeah, right, morphine. They gave me a Percocet, with no concern over the extent and intensity of the pain. I guess they all thought it was only a simple procedure that didn't even require an anesthetic, so what a crybaby I must be, and they left it like that. The "yeah, he'll be just fine, just give him an aspirin and call me in the morning" mentality prevailed with this place and the barbaric purveyors of pain that work there.

The entire episode was over by noon, and I was released from the hospital with not so much as a prescription for the pain. I had some pills, painkillers at home that I was taking, and I went home and tried to sleep. I didn't want to go to the doctor, and I thought I would be better soon. Unfortunately, it wasn't to be. I was lying down and getting up all that day and into the night with excruciating pain that wouldn't let up. I couldn't believe that I had a terrible toothache, loss of ability to digest food, not allowed to go to work, and now I was a twisted, convoluted bundle of flesh, writhing in pain, with no relief in sight. The hours passed by slowly, and I was comforted somewhat with the thought my wife and mother placed in my head, that all I had to do was get through the night and I would then get to go to see my doctor in the morning.

After possibly the worst night of my life, with no sleep and precious few moments with less severe pain, the dawn came through the window. Survival, hour by hour and sometimes minute by minute, I had endured the pain and could soon go to my doctor where relief was just a few more hours away. Unfortunately, it was like five thirty in the morning, and my doctor was probably still sleeping, and he was not going to see me for quite some time. I couldn't take any more pills. Besides, they didn't work anyway, with pain as severe as this.

So once again I had to battle time and pain, and try to convince myself that it would soon be time to see the doctor, and relief was within reach. I think I might have even fallen asleep for a brief moment or two, out of sheer exhaustion, I believe, but it didn't last long when the reality of this moment came rushing back with its pain and helplessness, along with the inability to do anything for myself.

During this morning's waiting for time to pass so I could see the doctor who didn't have morning hours, my wife called my boss to inform him of the path my life was going and that I had been to the hospital. He told her that I was terminated. Wow, I thought, more good news, but I couldn't even absorb or process such thoughts. Plus, I was still in pain and didn't care much about anything except relief.

Somehow it was noontime, twenty-four hours since I was discharged from the hospital. Actually I left without their official release because they weren't helping me with pain relief and I had pills and a bed at home. So the chance for some type of relief, I figured, was better at home, and I wanted to get away from this hospital that caused me so much pain. I was finally going to see my doctor. I'm quite sure I was annoying to anyone that happened to by chance cross my path that day. Those who cared for me were at their breaking point due to my inability to keep silent, with my pain, but I had been suffering for so long—pure hell it was, total consuming, gut-wrenching agony. I had called the office several hours ago, and they said I didn't have an appointment but if I wanted to come in that I could eventually see the doctor.

Imagine this. I'm suffering for over twenty-four hours and I have to bargain with the receptionist to get me in to see the doctor. We get there and I'm not holding back any outward revelations of my pain; thus, the vocal expressions of that pain and suffering was clearly evident to one and all that were unlucky enough to be in the waiting room that day. I even allowed myself to roll about on the floor occasionally to emphasize the desperation and dire straits I was in, foolishly hoping it would help me to get to see my doctor sooner.

I hear them call my name. I guess they got sick of seeing and hearing my suffering, or perhaps it was purely out of decency and kindness, but I was on my way into the office. I believe it was my shouts for help and the cursing and damnation of life and the inefficient and barbaric medical age in which I reside, but I was at last going to get relief and perhaps an explanation of why I was having so much pain from a supposed simple procedure with a small chance of some discomfort. I felt a sense of relief just knowing I was going to see my doctor. My pain had actually subsided briefly, just knowing I would soon be fine, as soon as I saw my doctor.

No human being is supposed to suffer relentlessly, like I had been suffering. There was now an end in sight to this nightmare, and all would be well again. I thought about the toothache I had had, and I couldn't imagine what it felt like. I was unable to place myself mentally into any spot but the *now*. The knowledge that I would soon be without the awful pain actually took it away for a spell. After the worst night and dreadfully eternal day of suffering I had ever experienced, I was now face-to-face with my primary care physician. At long last help and relief had arrived, and I was exhausted but grateful for having been able to get here.

Dr. Sklower calmly and systematically asked me all the relevant questions. Then without any hesitation and quite to my complete surprise, dismay, and disbelief, he said to get myself to the hospital, to the emergency room. The emergency room of the hospital that just inflicted upon me the worst pain I have ever endured. No painkillers, no prescriptions for any pills, no Oxycontin, no Percocet's, no fentanyl patch, no needles, nothing at all—just get myself to the emergency room. I think I was almost on my knees begging for some other method or means to restore my health.

Back to the hospital … damn. I had spent all night suffering, all the next morning suffering, dragged myself to the doctor, waited for hours, and only to be told no pills, no relief, get myself to the hospital. Damn. So it's back in the car. I'm filled with pain, and now I have anger to match the pain.

Why is all this happening, why can't I get some relief from the pain? So many questions, so few answers. Back to the hospital I go, the place that caused all this pain, back to the hospital, because the doctor said to go, and he didn't want me to have any painkillers (because something about masking any symptoms) until I went to the hospital ... back to the hospital, back to the source of all my pain. My God, is this but a dream, or just a nightmare?

Not much of a wait in the ER. I mean there wasn't any blood on me or any parts of me hanging off, or any of my bones sticking out, but they took me right quick. I guess it was due to my constant moaning and the haggard look of someone who had been suffering deep, excruciating pain for some length of time. So the good people took me right away into their world, the wonderful world of the ER, *where pain is measured by volume and remedy is dispensed sparingly.* Nothing but questions, and forms, confusion, pain, and aggravation—that was the scene. I had my own little room way in the corner, a sort of semi-isolation ward, I guess to keep me away from the other patients who seemed *neither to complain about the way they were being ignored or* the *pain that didn't ignore them.* I felt anger and pain. Dejection and anxiousness filled my every moment till I thought I would bust a blood vessel.

That's when an angel of a nurse came in to talk to me, kindness dripped from her lips, and like the angel she appeared to be, she whispered to me that she was gonna give me some morphine. Morphine ... just the idea of getting some or being told I was finally going to get some relief was a blessing, and I felt assured that my luck was changing and only good things lay ahead for me. I guess she realized and saw how much pain I was in. I didn't even feel the needle going into my vein, but I immediately felt the warmth that emanated from my back and neck and shoulders. Slowly the pain had subsided. I was in a trancelike state, not knowing why I was here, or even where here was, but not minding it at all, for the moment.

Maybe this was a good idea, to come to the hospital, after all I actually felt human again, with no pain. Then they started asking all kinds of questions about insurance and what was the reason for my being there, and the cause of my pain. Imagine this. They stab me with some type device to remove pieces of my liver while it's still inside me and then they want to know why I'm at the ER. So okay, I let loose with all types of verbiage about the butcher of a doctor that did the biopsy the day before and how I wondered if he was even a real doctor, or just a wannabe doctor. I asked what type of quacks and nutjobs they have that are walking around posing as doctors. Well, everyone was just pleased as punch with my insightful commentary, and we all had a nice chuckle or two, but I meant business. What kind of Dickensian nightmare was I an unwilling actor in?

They humored me as much as they could, I guess, and just wanted to pass me along to the next level of patient care, and maybe they imagined I might just disappear into the sunset. I know I wish I could get up and get on with normalcy. The pain had returned, and now they wanted me to go upstairs to get a CT scan. I suggested some more morphine might be more appropriate with my needs at the present time. Being overruled I insisted they give me more morphine. They retaliated stating it was too soon. I replied, "Tell my pain it's too soon, and who makes these idiot rules, all I want is some more morphine, please, thank you very much." I tried explaining that the amount put into my veins was the same amount they would give a 100 lbs woman, and I was a man over 350 lbs. Although the logic and the math were impeccable, the nurses rejected my reality, and it was off to radiology.

My next challenge was complying with the radiology staff's request for me to lie down on the section of the machine that glides in and out of the big magnetic donuts. The cradle or sled was extremely narrow, and they were adjusting pillows and rubber blocks to support me during the test. I was trying to rearrange these supports in a way that would not have me moving about once I became horizontal, as the additional discomfort of trying to raise myself up with nothing to push against seemed inevitable. They told me that they knew what they were doing and just let them do their job. I guess for most people just having to lie down wouldn't be much of a problem, but for me the task was monumental.

I might as well have been asked to climb Mount Everest. I have herniated disks for years that give me constant pain, especially when on my back, and now I have the additional discomfort, pain, and agony of a botched biopsy the day before on my liver. So I finally get onto the machine where I asked them if they were sure that's where they want me to lie, and no sooner does the searing pain start to subside from my Herculean effort when they ask me to lift up and slide your head back a bit. Can you imagine this! I told them to show me where they wanted me to lay on this thing as I won't be doing much adjusting of my body once I'm lying down. Then as soon as I breathe a sigh of relief, they want me to move. They were now talking to me as if I was a very bad little boy, patronizing me till I got more annoyed at their petty little platitudes designed to coerce me into some kind of submission, then the reality of my pain.

After this painful and humiliating ordeal to do this seemingly painless procedure, grimacing with pain, and angered by the unprofessionalism of the staff, I am taken back to the little room in the back of the ER. I start to think this room is for troublesome patients, and I believe they think I'm just some type of annoyance, and if they put me in this room, I'll get discouraged and just leave eventually. But I don't. I sit on the edge of the bed, and my mom is sitting on the chair, telling me to let the doctors do what they need to do, and she tries to comfort me as best as she could, which I appreciate, but the pain and the amount of time spent here and at the doctors and being up all night is beyond some comforting words, and I sit at the edge of the bed and wait.

I ask for more morphine even though I know it ain't coming, and it's too soon, and I ask for a prescription for some painkillers before I'm let out of the ER when an attendant comes charging in saying he has to take me upstairs for a CT scan. I chase him out of the room and angrily tell him, "We did that already." I can't believe the inefficiency of this place. No sooner do they bring me back than they want to take me upstairs again. *You gotta laugh at this*, I thought. They'll never get me some relief. "More morphine," I shout out. "Give me some more morphine. I already went upstairs and had the damn CT scan. What I need is more morphine."

Now my brain is filled with hatred for this place, the doctor that did the botched biopsy, the nurses that won't give me morphine, my third-grade teacher, the jerk in high school that used to pick on me, the girls in high school that wouldn't go out with me, and my doctor that sent me back to this horrible place. I'm causing quite a bit of a stir in the ER when the nurse-angel comes up to me and states that they want to take another CAT scan because they saw something.

They saw WHAT. I was just there less than thirty minutes ago. WHAT could they have seen? What is wrong with these people, and why are they doing these things! I just want to go home now, the hell with the pain. I just want to leave. No, I'm not going upstairs for another CAT scan.

I get up, walk past all the beds and sick people, and go to the outside of the hospital, and start walking around. I want to leave, but the pain is incredible and my mother is still inside, and then the nurse-angel comes over to me and says, "Go ahead, let them do another CAT scan, and I'll get you some more morphine." Finally, someone with a good idea, so all right. I calm down and wait for them to haul me back upstairs to my good friends in radiology. Feeling somewhat embarrassed for all the commotion I was causing, I chalked it all up to the pain and thought that they had seen worse than me plenty of times and thought about getting the morphine.

Back upstairs they take me right from the elevator down the hall, around the corner, and bang through the door into radiology— no waiting around in the hallway, no waiting and wondering what's taking so long, nope. They wheeled me right into their little electronic sanctuary, and like ants on pieces of sugar on the sidewalk on a hot summer day, they swarmed all over me and said they have to put an IV into my arm to administer contrast. Wow, this is a bit different than a half hour ago, and needles again, damn.

Whenever I get nervous, especially at times like these, I tend to talk incessantly. I guess it's my way to work off all the fears and uncertainties that surround me, and I try to get my mind to not dwell on what's happening by rejecting the moment and substituting my own reality.

So I start asking, "Why am I here again?" "Did you forget to do this with the needle the first time?" "Did I move before?" "Did something go wrong?" "What exactly is this contrast stuff?" "Is this the last time I'm coming in here today?" and a dozen more questions, most without any real answers.

Anyway, they do this stuff all day and know how to "schmooze" the patient, evade the questions, and get you to lie still with some bad outcome if you move or pain if you move, so stay still and they'll get through you and on to the next poor slob.

So no insight or proper response to my interrogation, especially when I asked, "What did they mean when they said they 'saw something' that required me to be brought back up here, what exactly did you 'see' what are we talking about? Please give me some kind of answer."

But none of them stopped what they were doing. All they said were, "You'll have to ask your doctor. We can't tell you anything."

Imagine this, I thought, *they can't tell me anything about me, or why I'm back in this machine, and I'm supposed to relax, forget about the pain from my back and my side, and just ask my doctor and he'll explain everything … take two aspirins and call me in the morning.*

Into the magnetic donut I ride, and then a mechanical voice tells me to breathe in and hold it … then let it out. A technician asks if I'm doing all right through the same sound system.

I wish I could tell her what I really feel, but I mumble "Yeah, sure."

Breathe in and hold it … let it out. Okay, one more time, and we're going to inject the contrast now. You may feel some warmth in your arm and chest. Were they asking me if I approved or just trying to frighten me some more? Breathe in and hold it … let it out. This sled is riding in and out and in and out, and then it slides all the way out. Once again they swarm all over me, undoing the tubing, removing the IV, and helping me to get off the sled.

In less than ten minutes I have only a Band-Aid to show I was even here. There are smiles, and they turn away and ignore me like I was never there, never there twice, both times I felt their cold antiseptic indifference, as if they were only interested in the mechanical application of their jobs, with no regard for the patient, or the patient's concerns, or worse yet, no regard for the fear, whether shown by the patient or not, and believe me I had fear after they bring me up for a second look-see at what I don't yet know.

So it's off for another ride, bouncing off the walls and uneven floors, and back to my little room I am returned, done I hope with the CAT scans, and morphine injection time I hope even more.

I tell my mother how silly I think this has all become, and I'm glad it's almost over, and where is that nurse with the morphine, and I could sure use some sleep, when charging into the ER comes this doctor with his white gown, going a million miles a minute, making a beeline right toward this little room me and my mother are sitting in. He rushes past a plethora of sick people and the loved ones that are standing alongside them comforting them, past the nurses and other support staff and hospital personnel, around beds and partitions, and screeches to a stop about five feet away from me, and without introducing himself, because I've never seen him, without any introduction or simple little common pleasantries that are common in modern society, without any warning of what was to come out of his mouth, he spurts out, "You have a tumor on your kidney, you'll have to have it removed." Just as suddenly he leaves me with those cold words and starts to leave the ER.

"Wow, am I hallucinating from the morphine, what did he say?" I look at my mother, who is getting up to leave the room. I ask her, "What did he say?"

She says she has to go to the bathroom and continues out the room. What did he say?

I chase after him through the ER as he is rushing away, and I stop him and say, "What are you talking about?"

With about as much compassion as a rock, he says, "You got cancer. Call your doctor. He knows more about it," then walks away.

I think. I don't think I looked anymore at this pathetic excuse for a doctor. With hindsight now, I feel such disgust that a doctor acts in such a callous way, but at the time I was too shocked to care about the delivery of the news as it was the news that devastated me to the core.

So there I was not really sure if the morphine had made me hallucinate and hear those words, or if it was reality and cancer was now going to be my constant companion, infiltrating every corner and crevice of my being. Like a dream or nightmare that I couldn't escape from, I was instantly plunged into a reality I couldn't accept, a place where fear and pain and uncertainty were dominant, and a place where goodness and kindness were totally forbidden. I was in doubt and disgusted at anything that was said to me, meant to console me for what had just transpired.

Perhaps I will fall asleep from exhaustion, and the drugs, and awaken to a world of bliss. I start to slip into unconsciousness, and my mother states that she's leaving to get home before the traffic gets heavy and it gets too dark. I watch as she weaves her way past the other patients on her way to the door. I catch up to her, and she says she has to go. I tell her she can't drive, she's too upset, and I will call my brother to take her home.

She tells me she doesn't want to bother my brother and she is fine. I follow her outside the hospital to her car, and she fights me to get into the car to drive off. She backs up onto the sidewalk, and I get the keys out of the ignition. I tell her she has to wait for my brother before she can leave. She yells at me and curses and swears she will never speak to me again.

So here I am standing in the street, calling my brother to ask him to come take Mom home, arguing with Mom, who's still yelling at me to leave her alone, trying to accept what this doctor has just told me, realizing I have no job, when my wife calls and asks me, "How are you doing?"

CHAPTER 2

DOCTOR KNOWS BEST

My brother finally arrives to take my mother, who is confused but gives in to take the ride. Besides the stares of people who witnessed the recent events, all now appears normal. Buses are stopping to pick up and drop off people, cars are driving by, all quite the normal doings on the avenue where we are standing. Yes, all things are just as normal as can be, except for the unshakable and horrible sounds of that doctor telling me I got cancer, like the AOL voice that states when you've got mail. Normal is never going to be normal for me ever again.

I was admitted to the hospital that night, and I said my good-byes to my family and felt like I was probably going to be dead a lot sooner than I had always thought. I thought about crying but somehow didn't. I sat in a waiting room, and I couldn't read any magazines. The words and sentences somehow all said the same thing: "You've got cancer."

I found a pen and some paper and started to sketch something, anything. I looked out the window and started drawing the bleak, dismal view I had from that window and the bleak, dismal view I now had on life. I've always enjoyed drawing, it seems to relax me somewhat, and it usually helps me to think clearer, but not that night. I sketched a smattering of roofs and buildings, all jumbled together, nothing too extraordinary, just a grouping of some dilapidated structures, some garages and some homes that looked like they should all be torn down. I drew the wires that crisscrossed the streets and the lights that's shown from the streetlights and windows.

I looked at the drawing I had created, and it was mostly dark, desolate, void of color and life, and faceless and desolate, as was my life and hopes of a future. I had cancer. I was alone. I was in a hospital, filled with uncertainties, and the suddenness of these events was unfathomable. I hated feeling sorry for myself, but I did. I was mad and angry at my own body for doing this to itself. I started blaming myself and trying to justify the why of it all, but there is no reason, or justice, to a thing like cancer. I had no warning this was happening inside my body. Yesterday I thought I was relatively healthy, and today I am very, very sick.

The remainder of the night I spent pacing the halls and looking into the rooms of the sick people that were sleeping or moaning. I thought I would now become one of them. Fifty-four years old, I have cancer and death flooding my body, threatening my life, and I am supposed to lay down in a hospital bed tonight and go gently into the night. I had no idea how long I would be in the hospital, or how long I had to live. I tried to force myself to think about something besides cancer, something besides this hospital. I wondered how long this evilness has been growing inside me. I was in denial, denial that this was happening, denial that I was now a cancer patient.

The following morning my regular doctor, my primary doctor, came in and asked if I wanted to go home. Before the last word was completely out of his mouth, I was headed out the door. He informed me there was no reason to keep me for observation, or any other reason, so I might as well go home, relax, and think about what I was going to do first. He suggested a doctor for me to see, a urologist. I wasn't even sure what a urologist was, or what he did, but I was pretty sure it had something to do with cancer. I half amusingly said that out loud to myself. He told me I could leave as soon as I had a ride, and then left to make his rounds. I was able to leave … and go where, and do what? After they tell you you've got cancer, and you're in a hospital, where in God's name are you supposed to go? I called my brother, who picked me up and drove me home.

It was a short drive home, and I was mostly silent, as was my brother who also has cancer (*How awful*, I thought, *to have such things in common*) and had his voice box removed and has to speak using a device he holds up to his throat, producing an artificial machine-like sound. I only have memories of his voice since his operation several years ago. I was silent, but my mind was racing at such speeds it made me physically ill. I arrived at home and hugged my wife, and I allowed (as if I could have stopped it) myself to cry.

My wife was very positive and encouraging, as was the rest of my family with reassuring phrases like "You'll be all right," "We can beat this, modern medicine has made so many advances," but none of this positive stuff had any effect on me. I felt alone, even though I had my family with me. I felt cheated, I felt betrayed, I felt dirty ugly and filled with poison. How can this be happening? I felt as though people were talking to someone else, or I was in a dream, or I was being filmed for a candid camera show? I thought how scary it was that one word could change your whole outlook, change your whole life, change how you think about anything, and change what you want from life. Yesterday I wanted a new car, a boat, some new tools, and today I just want yesterday, before cancer became my ever-present companion. *Nothing will ever be the same again, never ... forever.*

Besides the pain I had from the botched biopsy, I had no complaints or pain, it didn't make sense, so I rationalized it was some mistake, they had the wrong chart, the wrong person, and something ... anything was possible and probable, anything but this. I have to regain some control over my mind; my brain has to start thinking logically, because for the last twenty-four hours or so, I have had no control over my own thoughts or emotions, just a nonstop flood of irrational pleading with myself and searching for any logic that may be left in my world. My body had turned against me, but I had to control my thoughts at least. I was going to try and keep myself as active as possible to keep from falling into the crevices of despair, and keep myself out of the bottomless pit of doubt and fear. I knew I had to try to direct the course of my life and recovery instead of letting events direct me. *At the very least, this gave me some meager sense of control, and possibly hope was not so far distant as it surely was now.*

It sounded good, sounded like a plan, which is what I needed, a plan … any plan. So now I have to start looking for a doctor, a special cancer doctor, and before it was too long, I had a plethora of doctors, specialists in fields I had hardly any idea what they did. I also had no idea of the outrageous number of tests that I would be subjected to, in the hopes of discovering just exactly how much cancer was inside me, and if it has spread and on and on—an endless decline into the world of the laboratory guinea pig.

OK, so I decide to do whatever the doctor says, because he knows best. The doctor tells me it would be best for me to have a laparoscopic nephrectomy—new words to add to my vocabulary, and some horrible connotation they bring with them. Then he says the tumor may be too big for a laparoscopic nephrectomy, and that's all he does, so I should see a different urologist. New words, new doctor types, and all this being said to me with a straight face—serious business, I guess.

Now I can add more worry to my big pile of worries: *"Too big of a tumor."*

This doctor thinks the tumor is too big, so he can't and won't do the operation. Wow, get it cut out, get on with life. Wow, an operation, with scalpels and blood and anesthesia, and pain. A new doctor to go see. This is adding to the anxiety level.

I had figured OK, cancer, see a doctor (he knows best), cut it out, get on with life. An acceptable plan, I guess. So after waiting all morning to see this doctor, a sporting enthusiast, and listening to him talk about the Giants with his staff, he finally allows me to interrupt his sporting conversations, allows me and my brother into his office. He cavalierly suggests that I see another doctor, and continues his praise of the Giants. I try to act interested in what he is saying, but I'm not that interested in sports for one thing, and I have a slightly more serious problem that precludes me from social intercourse about football.

I left with an even lower opinion of the medical people I was subjecting myself with. Surely, I thought, the next doctor I see would be better, maybe even kinder, but my expectations were lowering daily.

I later will consider this event low on my list of annoyances that the medical field will inflict upon this greenhorn lad. I chalk the whole thing up to the fact that the doctor knows best.

CHAPTER 3

THE DOC THAT ROARED

I make an appointment with a second urologist, Dr. Schuman, not because of his reputation, and I've heard so much about his work, but because he was recommended by the first doctor, and as the saying goes …

The next afternoon, I act as calmly as someone who was just told they have cancer and it may be too big to operate via the most current methods can possibly be. I look around the waiting room, filled with fear and dark imaginings. I wonder if everyone here is sick. Which ones are just accompanying their loved ones, which ones have cancer, does everyone have cancer, and who doesn't?

I give the receptionists my particulars and she copies my insurance card. I even manage to make small talk as she tells me to fill out the obligatory forms. I am given a pen and a broken clipboard, and I sit in the only chair next to the tiny little lavatory in the waiting room and enter my information. Wow, how did it ever come to this, waiting to be seen by a doctor I never heard of, a doctor, who specializes in something I'm not quite sure of, in the hopes he can cut some part of me out so I can live.

The waiting room is dull and old, with hideous drab paintings hanging crooked on the walls. The chairs and the floorboards squeak whenever someone gets up. I don't believe anything but the patients have changed in twenty years or more. There are doors everywhere with nurses or staff or doctors coming and going at breakneck speed.

I wonder where they all are going. I notice one door that is opened, and the nurse appears to throw something down the steps. I see this happen several times, and I assume they are feeding some monster or dragon that lives in the basement. I amuse myself and others by suggesting this out loud to all the other occupants. I tell myself it is a good thing that I can notice all this stuff and keep my mind from thinking about the only thing I can't stop thinking about.

At last someone asks me to come with them to a small examination room where they take my blood pressure and attempt to take my weight, but the old rickety scale doesn't go that high. She shrugs, I grimace, and she hands me a cup and tells me she needs a urine sample for the doctor. She tells me I can go in "here." Here being a tiny little smaller than small little area, way too small to call a room, that has a sink and a toilet wedged inside. I enter as she closes the door, waiting for me to complete her request for a urine sample. With great dexterity and extreme difficulty, I comply, exit, and hand her the container and remain speechless. She takes the specimen and tells me "the doctor will be with you right away. Have a seat in the doctor's office."

The office matches the waiting room and is filled with a lifetime of achievements. The walls are covered with diplomas, awards, family pictures, college and medical school diplomas. Shelves are covered with trophies, medicine-related stuff, seashells, kids' pictures, pictures of sailboats, and models of sailboats. Every square inch is covered. I look around at everything from my seated position, too scared to actually stand up and look closer, but I notice all the names are not the same on theses diplomas and awards. As it turns out, it is a family business, consisting of three brothers and a sister, all related and all urologists.

When I meet the doctor, my head is swarming with a hundred different questions, besides the ones about all these things about the office. Maybe I should be calm and ask politely about the picture taking on a sailboat, and ask him if he goes ailing—no … no … no.

I have spent the last twenty-four hours pondering what I should ask, weighing each question for relevance (aren't they all relevant?), which questions can help, which are born from worry, which can help. My mind is already anticipating answers to questions that I haven't even asked yet. Perhaps the doctor will tell me there was a mistake made and they're very sorry for the inconvenience. I promise out loud that I won't be mad if this scenario plays out.

Dr. S finally rushes in, all busy and like a mad scientist distracted from doing what he would rather do, and introduces himself. I start asking him if he's done a lot of operations, a lot of laparoscopic operations. He begrudgingly answers quickly, seemingly annoyed at my interest in my future medical endeavors. I start to ask details as to how this operation will proceed, how it will be performed. Not exactly the questions I wanted to ask, but I was beyond nervous and scared to the core, half doubting this was actually reality, and perhaps I was already dead, and this was some kind of pre-admittance to hell.

I sound somewhat disconnected with my questions to the good doctor, as if I am talking about someone else's life, someone else's cancer, but I am dwelling on every word the doctor uses to respond to my inquiry. Each little syllable is precious to me now, every little parsing of the words he is using are rebounding in my head. I am debating with myself the various meanings of the things being said. When the doctor said this, did he mean that or something else but just said that?

He kept snapping his responses back at me like it was a duel of some sort, but I continued trying to understand what was going to be done to my body to excise this cancer inside of me, and I was truly in a place in my mind that I didn't want to be in. I asked him how they were going to remove my kidney if the only holes he mentioned he would make were just one-inch incisions to insert the various implements to dissect the kidney.

Well, apparently I went too far because this little man snapped, jumped up from his desk, started pointing his finger in my face and lecturing me about how he was a great doctor and didn't want to be questioned by least of all me about his medical prowess. I remember him saying you can't drill me with questions about everything. I know what I'm doing, he insisted.

Well, that was the straw that broke the camel's back, and the pent-up fears and disbelief and pain came flooding out of me like a broken fire hose, and I just started crying and crying. Crying and at the same time explaining how just a day or so ago I didn't have any thoughts about cancer, how I had gone to the doctor with pain, who sent me to the hospital ER, then to one doctor now here, and all I want to do is be healthy and I can't understand any of this, and when I get to finally ask the doctor who will operate on me some questions, you yell at me like I did something wrong.

Well, what happened at the time that seemed like the second worst thing that ever happened actually turned out to be fine. This codger fellow who was just berating me and scolding me like a principal correcting a delinquent schoolboy came out from behind his throne-like desk, dropped his facade, and any pretentiousness disappeared as he placed his arm around me and apologized for the words he just spoke.

He seemed completely sincere and believable, even to me in my weakened violated and filled-with-sorrows condition. The doctor expressed how he was indeed upset with his actions and his behavior toward me and he was sorry he came across as being so mean. He said he wished we could start out fresh, like this never happened and he never said those horrible words to me, but first impressions only happen once.

I am 6'4" tall around 350 lbs, and I guess to see me crying like a baby would be quite a sight for anyone, but here was this consummate professional man, a doctor, with decades of experience nearly pleading with me for forgiveness toward his lack of a bedside manner. What choice did I have? I acquiesced and stopped crying.

I was completely drained emotionally, totally confused, not sure of what I was going to do next. So this doctor tells me not to worry, trust in him, and everything will be fine. Let's start fresh. OK, so I have been everywhere my emotions could possibly take me, and I am at the bottom of it all, so why not try and act like all is well, so I squeeze out a small smile and shake the doctor's hand and say "OK, Doc, what do we do now."

As it turned out, this doctor was the most confident person I ever met, thus his being upset at my endless questions, perceived by him as challenges, but only offered as some way by me to override the

41

ever-present fear, in a desperate attempt to regain some semblance of control over my very shaky existence.

He went so far as to offer me his private cell phone number after the operation and told me to feel free to call him at any time of day if I was worried about anything. In fact, he turned out to be a very lovely, kind, and thoughtful doctor, calling me himself several times during my recovery after the operation to see how I felt in between office visits. He even obtained a special-sized support band for me from the hospital when I mentioned I was having some pain and I had to hold my stomach in as I moved about. Nope, there's no denying the good doctor his props. I still look forward years later to going to his office for a visit.

I always wondered what the subject most talked about at the doctor's Thanksgiving dinner table was since all his siblings were urologists.

CHAPTER 4

THE PATIENT ROARS

The next few weeks have become blurred and unclear as to what occurred and when, but I had to go through endless testing, and prodding and bodily invasions of every conceivable type, before I would be allowed to undergo my laparoscopic nephrectomy with hand assist. Boy that's a term not in most people's vocabulary, but it rolls off my lips like water over the falls. I would learn more and more about what was going to happen to me as the weeks went by, and I believe it was my learning about cancer and staging and medicine knowledge of how it grows and multiplies that kept me from losing it. I have researched and read and subscribed to everything I can.

Some might say I have become obsessed, or possessed. I like to think I have become empowered with knowledge. Others may choose to stay in the dark and not think about it, but I know I can't just stop thinking about cancer. I have cancer, and that is just a fact, and by reading and research, I have found so many more facts. I have grown as a human. I have learned about the marvels of human cellular development and what sometimes goes wrong. I have learned how the body protects itself and how blood vessels form *(angiogenesis)*, and how cells die a sort of programmed suicide *(apoptosis)*, and it all is so incredible *that one has to believe in some Higher Power that has enabled all these myriad things going on in the body with or without our knowledge or approval.*

Day after day I was being tested. Sometimes I was scheduled for more than one test a day. Eventually I had to get a notebook, more like an appointment book, to keep track of where I was and where I had to be today, tomorrow, and boy what a lot of tests they had. The majority of tests were to determine the location and possible spread of any cancer, or what they call pre-admission.

Another new word enters the vocabulary: *metastasis*. Lovely sounding, but its use is never welcomed unless it is accompanied by some other friendlier words like "no sign of," or "no visible evidence of." All merely qualifying words to make the main course more palatable.

At one point I was told to sit in a plastic tube that had just enough room for the door to close. I far exceeded the capacity of this machine in any layman's view, but they pressed on, along with my knees, which were bent against the walls, and I could barely fit inside. I called it the Official Medical Suffocation test since they planned to suck out the air and measure how much effort I could get out of my lungs. I mentioned due to my size they might need a larger test apparatus or tube, or perhaps consider prorating the results to adjust for my larger-than-average girth. They assured me they would calculate the results based on my size and told me to "just keep breathing." I barely passed this test.

I remember the doctor pushing against the door to seal it as he told me to turn this way and that. The poor guy was sweating and struggling for at least five minutes, opening and halfway closing the door, checking the hinges. He finally got it secured, but had to reopen it because he forgot to give me some breathing device needed for the test. I think I may have been amused a bit during this test. Then they sucked out the air little by little, measuring lung capacity or something. Horrible test, but all was justified to me by the endless onslaught of the minions that work and slave to do the biddings of their masters. I digress.

Next I was off to a cardiac doctor for a stress test, but due to my diminished lung capacity, from thirty-plus years of smoking Camels without the filter, I couldn't be tested using normal methods. I suppose a treadmill was the normal means, but I was to be injected with a drug that would make my heart race as if I was being chased down the street by a viscous gang of pit bulls outfitted in gang colors. This test was crucial as it would determine if my heart could withstand the operation, and mine would turn out to be eight hours long.

What is typical for the stress test is to get your heart rate up so they can check your valves and pressures, usually with a treadmill, with all types of wires connected to various parts of your body to monitor various bodily functions, including pressures and flow rates and oxygen saturation of your red blood cells, and stuff I have still no understanding of besides a few pages they gave me with charts and lines and various numbers.

So due to my 350-plus pounds and 6'4" frame, and herniated discs, and COPD from smoking, I was not going to be a likely candidate for the standard stress testing via treadmill. In fact, I don't remember when last it was that I could jog without almost passing out. Lucky for me the medical profession has come up with a neat alternative to all that huffing and puffing and sweating on a treadmill stuff. They found an injectable drug that they can inject into you to simulate the desired bodily activity.

Since the first time I was made brutally aware of the fact I had cancer, I have become semi-addicted or obsessed with knowledge of my condition and methodologies used to treat cancers. I have found various support groups online like ACOR, and many videos showing various cellular functions that are affected by cancer, various functions reduced or even destroyed by cancer cells. So I was well aware of this drug that they planned on injecting into my blood stream.

I went to the cardiologist's office for the test with my loose leaf binder. On the cover was a diagram of the heart identifying all the parts, valves, and chambers. I asked if they planned on using a particular drug for the test to elevate my blood pressure, and informed them I would not allow its use as the FDA has recently issued a "Black Box Warning" against use of this drug.

The doctor came out, looked at my binder with the heart on the front, and said he was impressed with my knowledge and it was a good thing for patients to take some interest in their treatment. He told me that his office had just recently changed from that particular drug to another and I could be assured all would be OK. Some might think "OK, that's good," but what damn drug would they have used a few weeks ago before they stopped and changed to the one I would now get? Vigilance, constant vigilance, is needed with these people.

This indeed would not be the only time I have prevented harm to my body by some uninformed medical procedure that was currently in use and whose future results are questionable. I refer to use of injectable contrast during CT scans, which everyone is accustomed to, but my research reveals some damage, and perhaps destroying of the kidney can result through its use. Therefore, this one kidney patient will suffice with perhaps a little less resolution on my scans, but zero chemically induced damage to my remaining kidney is assured by eliminating its use.

Even the use of X-ray by CT scan has some potential harm. Excessive radiation from years of testing can be harmful or deadly to the remaining kidney resulting in either dialysis or transplantation. Both of the above mentioned aspects of seemingly beneficial modalities that are daily touted to patients by their doctors can be rather harmful, disruptive, and perhaps deadly. I recommend cautious use of any procedure, thorough understanding of potential risks associated with a procedure as the only road to travel. Thus, we can prevent ourselves from being human guinea pigs, prevent pain, and perhaps with the grace of God, even save our own lives

This just helps in my determination and self-interest with the realization that any doctor spends up to an hour on me and my health problems, whereas I spend all day, every day with my afflictions, and health problems. I may not have as much knowledge as these doctors, but I know way more about me and my condition than any doctor ever will.

Wow I really have digressed. They hook me up for the stress test with all manner of wires and skin patches and cabling draped across my body. A nurse administers the injection. Another stands by next to me with a hypodermic needle, the biggest I have ever seen, ready to administer a second drug designed to counteract the first drug, in case I have a heart attack or something. How completely barbaric, I thought, to induce near heart attack conditions with an injection, and just standing there in case the undesired results occur.

I feel the rush of heat inside my body, and my brain tells me how ironic if I die here from a heart attack, while getting a stress test, to see if I can have an operation that might go wrong a million different ways and kill me, all in an effort to get rid of the cancer that is killing me. The test goes on for some time, with the nurse on standby constantly asking if I'm all right. I assure her I'm fine just a little warm, and the test ends when she injects the second drug to normalize my BP, and then I'm disconnected from the machine.

After some time in the waiting room, I'm called inside to see the doctor who is being constantly interrupted during my time with him by phone calls and aides asking endless questions and asking for instruction from him. He is looking at all the resulting graphs and charts and seems somewhat confused or distracted when he mutters something about not being able to approve me for my operation scheduled the following morning. Now I ain't too thrilled about having myself cut into with organ removal, but I have gotten myself convinced this has to happen, so what is this doctor talking about?

I inform the good doctor. I use the term "henceforth" for all doctors, because despite our doubts at the time they must be good persons to dedicate their lives to helping others, so "good doctor" it is. I inform him that despite any concerns he may have about this and that, that I fail to see the benefit to me by not allowing the operation to proceed so as to protect the patient's health, and that without the operation there won't be any patient or his health to consider, for the patient will be dead, expired, gone, no longer a concern to worry over.

Once again a clear case of a doctor worrying about himself and his practice at the expense of the patient. I'm not really sure how he resolved his apprehensions. If in fact he agreed with me in the end or not, but he did eventually give his approval for the operation, and I think I agreed to see him after the operation. I never did.

CHAPTER 5

A REALLY BIG NEEDLE AND OTHER PLEASANTRIES

Then there was a test called the bone scan, the purpose self-explanatory, the means not so simple. It would be a test designed to use X-rays and radioactive substances to locate self-induced "hot spots."

An injectable radioactive substance was transported to the test area in a large lead box that looked like it has been around since the eighteenth century. It was shaped like a miniature coffin, and inside was this humongous hypodermic needle. I had not been primed for this test, nor was there anyone besides the test giver, Hans, and his sidekick, Igor, in the room.

I am not quite sure of their given names, but the ones I gave them seem absolutely appropriate. Hans was immaculately dressed in white hospital garb, stood about 7' tall, erect with big, bulbous eyes and a large square head with white hair, crew cut style. His loyal assistant, Igor, was a short hunchbacked fellow with jet-black eyes and hair, dragging his one leg behind him as he shuffled about at Hans's direction all the while trying to keep his oversized pants from falling down.

It seemed longer than usual for this test to start. Plus, the time spent waiting between tests all add up to a breeding ground for worry and fears. I thought at least I didn't have to worry about work because I was fired. I wonder why I never got a mental exam, because I was bordering on some psychotic brand for sure had anyone bothered to look.

Anyway, this radioactive isotope that would soon be cruising through my body was the most expensive thing you could imagine. I don't recall the name, but they told me if they scheduled your scan for 10:00 a.m., they had until twelve, and then they would have to throw it out because of its half-life and charge several thousands of dollars whether it was used or not.

I started to think of half-life of the drug that was now cruising my body looking to be absorbed by cancer cells, and that I had lived for what I thought was about half my life expectancy until the heartless doctor ran into the ER a few days ago to tell me and all within hearing distance that I had cancer and no life. Half-life perhaps, I would have lived half a life instead of a whole life because of cancer and all this worrying.

The injection was uneventful, no side effects. I guess I was sort of getting used to the prodding and poking about my body. The X-ray machine was slowly passing over my entire body, from head to toe as I lay on the table. I was only slightly concerned about this radiation, and the X-rays, and the fact everyone had left the room and was watching on a monitor behind some really thick doors. The hardest part was remaining still for so long so a viable image can be made.

Hans was a nice fellow who had no problems answering all my questions, a nice break from the usual medical folks I meet. I would see him and talk with him every time I went back to the hospital for scans. He never changed. He was like a fixture there, always working, always talking, and a really nice guy.

I asked Hans what he was doing every time he left and went into the room outside my test area, but he declined to respond, saying he couldn't and wouldn't say one way or the other about anything. After an hour or so, the test was done from head to toe, and I was told I could leave.

I said, "For God's sake I just lay here for over an hour worrying and trying to suppress any bad thoughts from my head hoping to be told nothing was found. Can't you please tell me if you saw any hot spots? I know you're not a doctor, but you've been doing this for twenty years. Please tell me if you saw something, please, anything.

I've been going through a lot lately, and I already know I have cancer. PLEASE."

When he pushed open the door to let me out, he told me he didn't see anything at all, no hot spots, good luck. I thanked him as he drifted back into his private room and I drifted on to the next testing area.

I don't know how many tests I had or even what they were all for, but I tried to keep some sort of count to all these things. Keeping a count and being aware of what each test was for helped to delude me into thinking I had some control over my escalating world, my journey into the wonderful world of medicine.

Sometimes I was alone, and other times I was accompanied by some combination consisting of my mother, wife, and brother to help to get through this. But you always have the cancer with you, and you never will be certain that it is gone from your body ... just wish I could occasionally get it out of my thoughts.

I was next scheduled for a chest X-ray. Well, I assumed this would be the definitive test since I smoked for so long and they already found cancer inside me. I was pretty sure there would be more showing up on this test.

My body was no longer on my side, and it had actually become my enemy. I had inside me a cancer that was growing, and being nourished by my blood and supported by my body, with each breath I took and with each beat of my heart. I was growing and feeding something inside me without my permission and until recently without my knowledge, and I wanted it gone.

How insidious and clever this cancer seemed to be, living and thriving using my energy to become stronger and bigger until it kills the host. How stupid it was also, and there must be some way to kill this beast—after all good always wins out over evil and not just in the movies either. I wanted it dead.

I hated this monster. I hated the cigarettes I smoked. I hated the chemicals I was exposed to in my lifetime. I hated the government that allowed all the pollution and carcinogens to exist in our environment and invade our bodies.

Now they were going to see just how much more cancer I had in my lungs. I thought I was going to start this war against cancer on another front, but the lung X-ray showed nothing (unremarkable). I marveled at the creative ways, the simple and carefree ways, the doctors that evaluated the X-rays and CT scans would use to describe normalcy in such terms as to confuse the patient as to whether the test was good or bad. Maybe it was designed like this to keep the patient in the dark.

Unremarkable. Such uneventful tidings in their techno-world and such little nothings meaning just about everything to the recipients of these reports. It was truly enough to scare the daylights out of you until you can interpret the meaning behind their medically induced facade.

It meant just what the words said so very clearly, unremarkable, which is a good thing, a very good thing in this case, not like a musical concert, or a meal at a restaurant being unremarkable—ahh, the power of words, at their finest.

No lung cancer. Have to type that one twice.

No lung cancer, no hot spots, but heart not so good, ability to breathe not so good, but no new diagnosis, and we are now looking and searching my body piece by piece, organ by organ, to see what other hideous mutant cell life has developed over the fifty years I have ingested so many carcinogens, and been exposed to so many harmful substances. I guess you just keep on trucking through life oblivious to the harm you're causing until the brakes get jammed on when they tell you you've got cancer.

EKG, EEG, CT w/without oral/injectable contrast, X-ray, bone scan, ultrasound, stress test, lung and heart tests, blood and urine analysis and now I'm on the fast track for my laparoscopic radical nephrectomy with hand assist.

It resounds in the cavernous halls of a large cave and traverses the vastness between mountaintops and valleys, from the deepness of a low-pitched whale call to the nervousness of a jungle monkey communicating danger approaching, to an ocean liner moaning out its location to a nearby iceberg the ever-present words from a doctor in the emergency room so long ago: "You've got cancer."

CHAPTER 6

NEXT PLEASE OR X MARKS THE SPOT

I'm told to prepare for my operation with a clear liquid diet, and I have to drink this stuff to clean out my bowels, but I keep insisting that just telling me I had cancer did that already … right out of me. So out the window go any chance to relax my mind and try to forget about the operation for a day or so or a few hours. Every time I sit down on the toilet bowl and relieve myself I know why this cleansing is being done and soon I will be going to the hospital.

My wife and my family try to make life as normal as possible with talk about the weather, politics and what sales are coming up in the stores. I try and pretend some semblance of interest, and act like I hear what they are saying, but like a steamroller and a sledgehammer, my thoughts are only of the pending operation.

I look at my watch … less than twenty-four hours to go. Maybe I can postpone. Maybe the planet will stop spinning and this will lose its sense of urgency. Maybe the phone will ring with the hospital calling saying they are terribly sorry but there was a terrible mistake and someone put my name on a cancer report, and they're sorry for the mix-up and all the worrying that goes with the cancer, but not to worry, the person has been reprimanded and fired. Rightfully so, I reply, but alas, reality bites.

No, I have to get this thing done now. I try to relax again. I can sit and watch TV for hours and not see or hear anything but my thoughts and my imaginings about what is about to happen and how did it ever get to be this. What if something goes wrong? My God, there really are so many things that could go wrong.

Sleep—I must get some sleep. The thought of sleeping scares me as much as an operation does. I hate nightmares and dreams when some horrible chore awaits me the following day. I contemplate a sleeping pill, but I don't have any. Eventually I fall asleep, and I dream of "Pac Man" eating my cancer, which I explained to my oncologist. I wake up and fall asleep several times that night worrying and feeling very sorry for myself. I consider it normal and get through the night somehow.

Somehow the time passes and I'm inside Christ Hospital. The nurse is preparing me, and I'm not being polite or even helpful. I guess I was sort of taking things out on this poor innocent creature. She's only asking me simple questions to fill out her admittance forms, but I still give her a hard time with this. She finally tells me I don't have to be this way, and if I don't want to have her help me, she'll stop and I can go home. What a terrific idea, just get up, I can still walk all right, and go home.

Later on, after my operation, this same nurse visits me on four different occasions in two different rooms and floors, the ICU and my own recovery room. An angel, for sure, had blessed my way.

Although the immediate benefit of giving in and getting the hell out of the hospital appeals to me in so many ways, the least of them being no scalpels and blood and pain, I acquiesce to my more educated and wiser self and proceed with the admittance procedure minus the pain in the ass I was being. Yup. I decide to take it like a man and adopt the "let's do it" attitude so appropriately displayed years ago in Montana by Gary Gilmore when he was sentenced to hang.

I get all fitted up with air bladders on my legs to force the blood into my chest during and after the operation. My wife helps me with the flimsy hospital garb and places my street clothes in a bag provided by the hospital and into some little locker on the wall. I'm thinking, *Wow, I'm really gonna get this done, no reprieve from the governor, no last-minute 'Stop, this is the wrong patient' from some on the ball secretary who picks up the mistake, no end of the world instead of this.*

Into my bed and everybody is being as courteous as can be talking about anything but why I'm here. I wanna scream out "This sucks. Last week I was eating hamburgers watching TV and worrying about what grass seed to use on the lawn, not my health, cancer, and an operation."

Finding myself worrying more and more and I try to find an end to the worrying when it finally dawns on me: "What If They Take Out the Wrong Kidney." My God, that's why I was worrying of course. I must ensure the right one is removed, but the left kidney is the right one (correct one). Besides if the doctor is standing above me, his right is my left. This is my only concern before the operation, as I fear and imagine having a remaining kidney that needs to come out because they took the wrong one.

I am completely obsessing with this notion now and what if I mention it over and over and the doctor says "OK, he said the right kidney," but did he mean the right side was the right kidney to remove? Or the doctor thinking it's his right, which is my left. I was on to some big-time problem here for sure, and I knew it had to be resolved before anybody cut anybody, especially me.

Mostly everyone thought I was worried for nothing when my mother said have them mark it with a magic marker. I thought and rejected the idea almost at once.

As soon as Dr. Schumann heard my ranting and worrying, he came over, lifted my gown, and made a big X on my abdomen saying "There now you can be sure we'll take out the right one" What a great doctor, I thought, and Mom.

Dr. Schumann greeted all that were assembled at my bedside and assured me of a positive outcome and told me that all I had to do was go to sleep and him and his team would take care of everything.

I said my goodbyes and told my mother I was scared. She said she would see me after the operation and "don't worry, everything will be fine," which is what she always says about everything. Good way to be, I realized, unlike my worrying if the sun will rise today.

Away I went on my back down the hall staring at the ceiling tiles, through the door, and into the OR. I don't know how many hospital personnel were there, but there was a lot. I started talking to whoever would listen, saying I was sure they were all highly skilled and they were going to do a good job, followed with right? (Awaiting reply.)

Dr. Schuman came up and touched my shoulder and said, "Relax, look at all the pretty women in this room all here to take good care of you." Then they once again swarmed all over me for preparation for the doctors. Pillows and I were strategically placed; an IV was hooked up to my arm that was tied down, something being hooked up to my legs. I twisted and looked around as much as I could to see what I could see. Wow, lights, action, and cameras. This was a laparoscopic operation, so they did use a lot of cameras and monitors. There were trays with tools and packages and cables and white cloth and sheets and gowns and colorful hats and gowns on all the peoples around me.

They said they were going to put me asleep now, and that was what they did ... out. I slept through all the stuff you couldn't believe, catheter insertions, laparoscopic probes inserted, at five different locations, port incision to remove the kidney, a breathing tube inserted down the throat, waste removal catheter, straps staples and stitches, and everything else. Not once did they said they were putting me to sleep, but that's what I did, waking up in the post-surgery room, waking up, "Yeah, that's good," I fall back asleep.

I'm alive, I survived, wow ... I wonder how much morphine they have in my body ... I wonder if I can move ... wow, I better go back to sleep ... wow, I'm alive.

I hear some voices, unfamiliar voices talking to each other discussing how they're going to do whatever it is they're doing. They start moving me around, twisting and turning. I'm being maneuvered about by some pretty tough nurses who aren't going to let anything like 350-plus pounds stop them from their intended goal, whatever that is. I think they are trying to change the sheet or something, with me in it. I guess they achieved their goal, for they soon walk away from my area, still talking. I fall back asleep again.

I don't feel like I am connected to all my body parts. A certain separation anxiety takes over my semiconscious state, as I discover a tube coming from my penis that goes to a bag at the end of the bed. I guess so I don't have to get up to pee—thank God for that. I'm able to pee, I think, but I don't have the strength to pull myself up to see. I don't have enough strength to do anything, back to sleep.

Again these two tough Neanderthal nurses toss me about like nothing so they can do whatever it is they're doing, very forceful, very rough, without regard for the patient. I was being scolded for something and being told not to let it happen again, as they wrapped me so tight I couldn't move. I couldn't wait to get stronger so I can take these two gangsters on, but I fell back to sleep.

My penis is hooked up to a catheter, my arm has an IV in it, some type of clip on my finger, measuring oxygen in the blood of all things, and some rubber bladders wrapped around my legs to keep blood somewhere, or for maintaining pressure. But I allow the clip on my finger to "fall off" whenever I need the nurse's attention. Because it sounds an alarm and they charge in when they hear it. They figured it out and told me they wanted me to press some switch if I needed them and they wouldn't bother with the clip on my finger anymore. It was just a case of me having some semblance of control, regardless of how menial it truly was.

So my lower extremities are hooked up to an air line, tubes all over, and they got me all wrapped up like a bug in a rug, not in a room, but right next to their station, so they can keep a close watch on me. The only thing I ever do is go back to sleep. Every time I wake and take stock of my condition, before I can get some answer to whatever I'm mumbling, I go back to sleep.

Not knowing how long this went on, probably about a day, I thought I was stuck in that place for a week. My wife was allowed to see me in this post op area, and she tells me I was mostly incoherent and I kept trying to get out of bed and the nurses kept me secure with tight blankets and sheets. I remember trying to ask somebody something, but there was nobody there, and then when someone was there, I couldn't get the strength to get the words out, so I just went back to sleep.

I overheard my Russian jailers, the Pillsbury dough boyish nurses, saying they were going to show me as they were working on me and my leg bladders. Apparently I had somehow worked my way free of these constraints in my quest for freedom, and these two were of a singular obsession to get these bladders reattached regardless of any discomfort it caused me.

I complained a lot about those bladders and my inability to do anything. In fact, all I could do was complain, and as long as I was awake, I complained. I guess I was a bad patient at the post op area, but these nurses were harsh, domineering, and determined to get done what they were supposed to, as quickly as possible so they could get back to their soap operas on TV, or get back to plucking out their facial hairs. They were not sociable and had no intention of babying me or putting up with anything that interfered with their goals, no matter who cared about it. When I wanted a tissue or a mouthful of water, I had to beg and get their attention, however I could. It seemed like the last thing they wanted to do was make my time there easier, or help me when I needed it most.

I asked when I was getting out of here, and they told me "as soon as we can find you a room." I said it wasn't soon enough. I guess that kind of pissed them off because they wheeled me into a room inside the post op that could be isolated enough that no one could hear any cries of pain or begging for the simplest of things to help survive the ordeal. I mean like a pillow out of place that's actually bothering you, you have to call a nurse; a box of tissues an inch or so placed in the wrong spot and you have to ask a nurse to move them closer; and you can see how they get all annoyed over such simple little things. It becomes so frustrating at times, because if the nurses are nice you don't want to bother them, and if they're mean, they won't let you bother them. Either way you lose.

A different set of nurses was on duty, and I overheard them say that a room had become available. Eureka. I immediately started to get myself ready without any approval or permission. I figured I would make it easier for them to move me, and quicker if I started things off myself. So I struggled and struggled to get the damned rubber bladders off my legs, and somehow after a tremendous effort,

I was successful in removing them. I also got the sheet and blanket off as well, and I was sitting there ready to get moving to my new room and feeling tired but proud of my ability to help myself when the nurse comes in.

She starts complaining about this and that and what the hell do I think I'm doing. I tell her I was trying to help get ready for my move to a room, and she tells me there is no room available for me yet and we have to put all this stuff back on you. She starts scolding me and saying bad boy as I lay there uncooperative as they blow up the bladders and stretch on the leggings, regardless of the discomfort all this activity is to my weakened (just out of surgery about twenty-four hours ago) condition. So I back down from my anticipated removal from this place and readjust my thinking as to surviving until strength returns. Then I go back to sleep with all my tubes and straps in place and my keepers still plucking facial hair.

"At last, his room is ready," I overheard my keepers babbling. Then they came into my area like gangbusters, unchaining me from my granite slab, connecting and disconnecting all manner of devices designed to keep me as a semi-invalid incapable of the simplest movements. I was now reattached to a portable slab to convey me to my next destination, with devices attached that beeped and buzzed. All of this was conveniently covered with a sheet so no one knew what was being wheeled by them as I journeyed to my newest abode, my own room.

Other slabs parked along the side of the road as if they were broken down and they were awaiting car service. I am not impressed by the joyous attitude of my driver as he crashes into walls and corners and his caviler attitude when he shouts out "Oops sorry 'bout that," and bangs into the not quite fully opened elevator doors. I'm not complaining as this is indeed more tolerable than the morbid atmosphere that I am escaping from. I simply point it out in case an investigation is mounted and I am called to testify, just for the record that's all.

I get a glimpse during my journey through the halls at many other sick people, and I am once again humbled by the experience as

I reflect upon my own condition and how much better off I am than some others who will die during my stay or shortly after. I also think about the children suffering, and I sober up and thank God I have been spared such tragedy up to now.

Delivered to my room all safe and sound and I start to take stock of my present situation and what I can do to improve my current lot in life. After all I am alive. So I ask the nurse when can I get this tube removed from my penis as it is uncomfortable and even painful during any tossing and turning I do, which is about all I am capable of doing anyway. She replies that she'll remove it right away, but if I get any pee on her bed, she's putting it right back in, and in case I forgot, the first time it was placed in me I was under anesthesia; the next time I won't be.

Eventually I asked to have it removed because of the damned bag hanging at the foot of my bed letting everyone know I was peeing or asking someone to empty the container, and it was starting to hurt, and I figured I could easily just as well get out of bed, walk the few feet to the bathroom if I had to pee. As soon as it was removed and everyone left, I stood up and fell right back down, no strength in my body to support myself standing.

Wow, I thought, what a mess I got myself into. I eventually managed to brace myself against stuff and get to the bathroom to pee, and managed somehow to get back to bed and collapse, but I kept having trouble with the IV that was in my hand and the cart that carried the bottles of saline and medicine. It was a real workout to move less than ten feet back and forth to the bathroom, made me think I would be handicapped for life.

The third or fourth time my IV fell out, it took several tries by several nurses and the house doctor before they got it in correctly, and when they finally did it, they ensured it would stay in with tape, tape, and more tape. In fact, every time a nurse was in the area, she would stop in and look at my hand and place some extra tape to ensure it stayed.

In fact, I stole some tape from one of the little trays they bring in when they check you, and I spent the better part of a whole day taping the hand. It was rather difficult since I couldn't use my hand or move it much, but I didn't want them sticking and sticking me again to get the damned IV in my hand. I think I had several rolls of tape at one point just in case, but unfortunately they soon removed the IV and said no more morphine.

Talk about fear. This morphine pump was like a lifeline to life. For two days, every time it would reset itself (a couple of hours I think) I could press the button to get pain relief without bothering any nurse, at any time of the day or night. Perhaps it was the reason I constantly feel asleep whenever I woke up. In any case I can't imagine being conscious right out of major surgery without this device.

One of the perplexing problems besides all the physical, mental, spiritual, and physiological crap involved in getting yourself from point A (pre-knowing) to point B (knowledge) is the realization that you can't possibly get it all right. There's just too much involved. That's why God created such wonderful creatures as the nurse. I will continue my story, but find I have to take this opportunity to relate one of the least comforting episodes I have ever endured. I have devoted the following chapter to this, with hopes it may soon escape my memory and reside it to the junkyard of human unkindness, selfish motivation, and apathetic indifference.

CHAPTER 7

I MUST BE CRAZY

I have forgotten to mention in my previous entries that my operation, my kidney removal, was done without ever seeing or being told to see, or consulting with an oncologist. At the time I gave it no thought, but today recalling the events of years ago, I am shocked that I didn't seek out and find a competent and caring oncologist before I did anything major like an operation to remove an organ from my body. Fact is, never got a second, or third opinion, because I wanted the cancer out of me as soon as it was approved with all the myriad testing by the hospital for pre-admittance and the insurance approval. I wanted this uninvited growth removed.

At times, during my first learning of my cancer, I hated my body and didn't care what would be done because it, my body, had become my enemy. I felt like my own body was trying to kill me, and the truth is that it was. Cancer cells that were in me were still me. Deformed mutant cells, but they were still me. I thought if you have a deformed child or a Down syndrome baby, only evil people kill it. The rest accept their gift from God and do all in their power to give the child a life to be proud of. So why did I have this thing inside me and the host itself. I was indeed a mess. I will continue now with my story.

All I had learned on the Internet, and my gut feelings were in agreement that I should seek out and go see a cancer doctor, an oncologist, a doctor that specializes in cancer. What a horrible job that must be when all your patients are suffering from cancer. Everybody you see will probably be dead shortly, will probably not get better, and why would anyone do a job like that? I suppose helping people so sick is a noble calling, and it can be very satisfying to help those who most need help. Then again how fulfilling it must be to see someone cured of cancer, or it not spreading due to something the doctor did.

I rationalized all types of various scenarios to better understand what type of person I was going to subject myself to in this vast wonder world of the medical arena that was still unfolding and revealing itself to me. I kept thinking of the bald-headed children you see on TV when they discuss cancer and radiation and chemotherapy, and I couldn't imagine the stress of seeing this each and every day.

With all these images and emotions swirling about inside my head, I was off to see my oncologists, recommended by one of my doctors on the growing list of specialists that I now had to help me on my journey with the beast.

A petite, frail-looking creature with black hair tied back in a bun on top of her head, dark eyes behind thick black glasses, and a heavy accent that added to the intrigue surrounding her as we met. There was suddenness to her every move and an obvious desire to "let's get going" here that I noticed from the first moments of our meeting. She started to ask me a litany of questions from a book she had, and I felt like it was such a bother for her to be asking the same questions over and over, as if I was just a routine she had to go through, not unlike taking a crap in the morning.

Sudden thoughts to apologize for that last line, but since it is so apropos to the situation, it must, by rights, remain. In addition, it was easy to see how truly uninterested she was in the questions she asked or in my responses, as there was never enough time to answer when she went on to another question. I felt my limited patience being stretched like a rubber band, and I hoped it wouldn't snap.

This was not the way I thought it was going to be, but neither has anything else gone close to expectations, so I just continued. Every time I tried to ask her a question, her slender, bony finger would jump up out of her gnarly fist, and she would place it against her lipstick-encrusted, shriveled upper lip, close her good eye, and say in a tone like she was talking to some school boy, "Just answer the question please."

I suppose this charade of her feigning interest and myself pretending she cared went on for fifteen minutes before she actually started to answer any of my questions: questions which were usually deep, penetrating excursions into the reasons behind accepted practices and questions about why things were done as they are. I have had this trait since boyhood, and it has never fared me well, but it is hard to change when you have been doing something for so long, regardless of consequence. Besides, there was an enormous amount of things I needed to know, and I could see that there ain't nobody freely giving up anything on their own in this profession, so I keep slugging away to get some valid responses from all these smarter-than-me people, but I digress.

Vigorously trying to explain to her how I felt and what I thought my body was doing, believing that a doctor can treat the patient better if he knew what the patient was feeling. She was not interested in what I was saying. She was just waiting for me to stop talking, and she had the audacity to say to me that she was the doctor and I was the patient, and don't worry. It was like I was a very bad school boy and she was going to correct my bad habits. Habits like trying to explain my feelings to someone in the medical profession I thought would most care about such things, a cancer doctor. Perhaps no one cared; they were just doing a job.

I was now at an even lower level than I thought possible when she asked me if I wanted to be in a clinical trial and she mentioned about five-year survival rates, and wow, I thought, the cancer was removed, so what's with this five-year survival stuff? She started going into some explanation of it, but my mind had shut down to her voice. I was zoned out. I mean I could still see her talking and gesturing as if she was taking a nice walk on a tree-lined path around the lake, in the park on a sunny summer afternoon. But all I heard was a five-year survival rate, as opposed to what a five-year death rate, and what happens after five years? Does anyone survive after five years?

63

Did I just hear her say "I at least can expect or hope to be alive for five years"? How did they come up with five years? Why not five years plus five more years, and call it the ten years' survival rate? I was really shaken by this latest unexpected attack on my being, what's left of my body, and for sure what's left of my mind.

Somewhere in here I mention to her that the doctors that took my kidney said I wouldn't need any chemo or radiation, which I thought was a rather good sign, and that my overall prognosis was excellent considering both the operation, and the doctors' not recommending chemo and such. She spits out sort of sarcastically that she agreed with my doctor but only because they won't have any effect on my cancer. No effect on my cancer, she relates that chemo and radiation are for me useless and not worth the bother. Still she is asking if I can join a clinical trial with experimental drugs that have some very nasty side effects, like puking and diarrhea and hair loss and skin irritation, and I won't mention worse. I thought to myself what a pesky little arrogant creature I am dealing with. Okay, spit it out, doc, what else didn't I know?

She glanced at her book and looked back up at me and asked if I would be interested in the clinical trial she talked about, adding that she would need my answer today. I said I would need more time so I can research this idea. This seemed to really annoy her, more so than everything else I said that she didn't like, as if I existed merely to satisfy her morbid curiosity in sick people, like I was just a cancer person, but I might just as well have been a leper.

At some point I got her to listen, by asking if I could just tell her something, and could she just be quiet and listen to what I had to say. She placed her pen down on the book on her lap, lowered her glasses down her nose, stared directly into and through to the very back of my eyes, and said in a shrieking voice like chalk on a blackboard, "Go ahead, what do you have to say, come on, get it out."

"We don't have all day. And I still have paperwork to fill out on you." Like the bad witch in the Wizard of Oz, frightening Dorothy and millions of viewers over the years. I had come face-to-face with the wicked witch, and this sure wasn't Kansas anymore. I began to tremble in my shoes and knew full well clicking my heels wasn't getting me out of here.

I first asked her what she thought about "Targeted Therapy" because it was one of the complimentary therapies that I had read about and I was interested in its degree of effectiveness. Besides, it seemed like such a promising area of research and treatment. Before I even finished describing my interest, she started shaking her head back and forth and waving her pointed gnarly index finger about as if I were asking if I could borrow her Mercedes and cruise around town for a spell and saying, "Nope, I don't believe it, I don't believe in any of it." "What else do you have to say?"

Not yet completely dismayed by her less-than-enthusiastic interest in me or my welfare, I continued with another question about Guided Imagery. I decided to tell her that I was able to imagine my white blood cells as tiny little "Pac Man" figures, and that they were swimming about in my blood, attacking, eating, and spitting out pieces of the bad black cancer cells. I stated that it seemed like it was an area of potentially great scientific interest for all those interested in eradicating cancer and that it was in my opinion a viable complementary means of treatment to go along with the pitifully small, miniscule, but accepted, methodologies of treatment available for RCC today, which she had so callously reminded me off. She sat there face contorted, squirming in her tiny chair, looking as if I was from another planet, or should be on one.

I further explained what I thought was a pretty clear view of the current field of medicine pertaining to kidney cancer by explaining again my knowledge that due to RCC's known nonresponsive action to both radiation and chemotherapy, there was a vast interest in complementary methods to treat both patient and the disease like aromatherapy, music, and yoga, acupuncture, diet, and stress factors.

All in all, I thought I had made a great commentary about the subject and showed my interest in my own recovery, and had mentioned about my increasing interest in all these various means to treat the beast. I was feeling pretty good about it all, especially when I mentioned about the "Pac Man" eating my cancer, and was anxiously awaiting some semblance of decency and respect from this shrill excuse of a doctor.

Hippocratic oath be damned, this tiny creature stood up all five feet of her and got closer and closer to me, looked me dead in the eyes with such intensity, and spit out in no uncertain terms, "WELL, maybe you should be seeing a psychiatrist instead of an oncologist." Then she turned around and walked out of the room.

I could barely believe that this was a response from a doctor to a cancer patient who was trying to express his fear and concerns to a cancer doctor. Talk about bedside manner. Needless to say, I left and never went back, but when they sent the bill, I wrote "Patient deceased" and sent it back. I left that day with more doubts about my health and my sanity. I questioned my approach toward treatment and my medical options, and I even questioned my questions. I wondered if some of them were rational or even if they were relevant … but weren't they all relevant?

I supposed that I had somehow wandered into a reality zone that was quite totally different from anything I had ever imagined. I felt as if a stranger in a foreign land might feel when lost and unable to communicate or get directions. Only difference was they knew where they were going. I didn't.

CHAPTER 8

EVERY DAY IS A GIFT

There I was, ensconced in my own room, and one of the first things asked for was a sky hook. I wasn't sure anyone knew what it was, but this nurse from another floor overheard me and had an orderly hook up an overhead bar with a large triangle on a length of chain. It was exactly what I needed to position myself whenever I needed to without asking for help, which came sporadically at best. It was a bit of independence in a world dominated by dependency. This nurse was also responsible for bringing me what she called the cardiac chair, a great big recliner that takes up half the room, another great piece of independence. What a wonderful nurse. I imagined what it would be like if I was her patient, and I even tried to get myself transferred, but she was a maternity nurse, so not much chance of being her patient.

I was visited by the doctors, who would stop in, say who they were, say I looked good, and several weeks later submit an outrageous bill for the interruption of my recuperative resting. I was visited by nurses, most of whom were genuinely concerned with my condition and did whatever they could to make the unbearable tolerable, and to allow an unhappy patient a chance to break out with a smile.

I was also visited by my family, which was a blessing, but I spent the majority of my time by myself with my pain and my endless thoughts about everything horrible that could happen to me and how bad could anything really be because the only reality I had was that I was in a hospital and I had cancer.

Whenever anyone was about to leave, I would ask them to get me a glass of water, the tissue box, and the switch to call the nurses. I would have them close enough for me to reach, which was only a matter of inches before pain set in. Without exception, every time I reached for anything, the tissue box would somehow fall, either off the bed completely or just enough to be out of reach. Either way I had lost access to it.

Boy how I needed that box of tissue for removing all the mucous that would accumulate steadily in my mouth. It was like my only connection to my life before the cancer surgery. It seemed such a little necessity would be not so hard to have, but it became an hourly challenge to keep a box of tissue near me at all times. I tried so hard to keep it within my reach, but to no avail. Over and over I would summon the nurse, who seemed annoyed that all I called her for was to pick up a box of tissues from the floor, as if I was doing it on purpose.

So sometimes I wouldn't call the nurse but tried to get it myself, suffering unimaginable pain. But I tried, and sometimes the nurse would come in and place me back into position on the bed, cover me up, and place the tissue box on the little table they had for eating on, close enough to see, but it might just as well not be in the room. So she believes that she was helping me, and now I'm all tied up in the bedsheets unable to move, and the tissue is farther away than before.

This went on until I had acquired several tissue boxes, which I had strategically placed at various locations to facilitate my usage. I had boxes under the pillow, under the blankets, on the table, and on the bed at several locations. When they made up the bed, they would take all the boxes they found and place them on the radiator cover on the other side of the room, despite my pleading and begging.

This tissue war with the nurses, acting like I was doing these things on purpose, and acting like I was spoiled and it was beneath them to pick up the tissue box, call an aide, or do something for me, had completely dominated my time and thoughts. I even started to think I was overreacting or going nuts. I would try to stretch out my leg and hear a box fall on the floor. I would reach over to remove a tissue from a box on the bed, and it would unhesitatingly fall to the floor. Seemed like every time someone came in the room, after they asked me how I was, I would ask them to get my tissue box.

Being in this room, recovering from major surgery, the simplest of things become major events or tasks. Before my hospitalization, I never even used tissue. Now they were on the level of air and water and food.

Another major event is when they bring food. It was about the third day that I attempted eating. They brought in chicken broth, with no chicken, tea no milk or sugar, and Jell-O. The portions were childlike, and I fell asleep after sipping some broth and drinking some sips of water. Looking at the food, I wondered why I wasn't being fed any solid foods. They informed me I wouldn't be getting any solid foods until my bowels started to work again.

What did that mean, when they start working again? When did they stop working? Great, something else to worry about! I was told that basically my body's digestive system was shut down for the operation, and they didn't want to put anything in unless they were sure it was going to be coming out. And as far as they were concerned, the best way to determine all was in working order inside me was for me to pass a fart. Yes, they actually told me no solid food until I farted.

Well, damn I was good at that, and could even play simple melodies after some hot dogs and beans. No problem, doc. But I didn't have anything in me but water juice and broth. I waited and waited, and they would ask if I was "ready" for solid food yet, and I honestly replied, "No, I haven't farted yet." It was starting to trouble me, and I thought what would happen if my digestive system failed to start back up, what if there was no fart, would I be on liquid diet till the day I died? Yet another worry coursing through this mind trapped inside this cancerous vessel.

I remember trying so hard to do something that used to happen on its own sometimes without expectation or want, yet here I was perhaps going to starve to death because I could not do something that everyone frowns upon. I was to be denied sustenance because of the inability to pass some gas. Preposterous. I decided I was going to fart, and nothing short of a heart attack would stop me.

One day someone was cleaning up the room, a volunteer I believe, and as I turned to see who had just entered my room, I farted. I let out a long, loud fart, probably the best fart I ever did. It was a long time in the making. The lady in the room looked at me, sort of embarrassed, and then turned away as if she didn't hear it, and kept on doing what she was doing.

Immediately I called for the nurse, and when she arrived, I proudly boasted of my latest accomplishment. I said to the volunteer, "Tell the nurse, you heard me fart, right?" Encouraging her honesty, she finally acquiesced and admitted I did, though she looked as if she was betraying some trust or something. I assured her it was quite all right to tell, and now I would be able to eat solid food. A great leap forward had been made in my recovery from the operation that removed my kidney along with the cancer.

I was becoming aware of how so many of life's functions go on without anyone having to be aware of them or to even have to think of them. I had just spent the better part of the day concentrating on my digestive system, trying to actually control it with my conscious thoughts and trying to bring about by sheer willpower that which occurs naturally without even a thought given to its successful completion. I was becoming more aware of self and starting to have appreciation of all that we take for granted every day and every moment we live. How much clearer things now appeared! So much awareness of life was now made known to this temporarily bedridden soul. It was like an awakening had occurred.

I started to think that how incredible this cancer was, that an errant mutation of a cell was so darn determined to live that against all the odds, and all the myriad safeguards, that are in our bodies to defend against such an onslaught, that it was able to survive in a world that was dead set against its survival. My immune system had failed and allowed this cell to become a dominant part of me. Yet I still thought that even this cancer cell was actually a part of me, so how could the immune system recognize it as an enemy and attack it?

For as bad as the terrible child is, he is still our child and our flesh and blood, so we don't kill our defective offspring but attempt to correct and control, which is how I was starting to look at my own cancer cells, my own body, trying to destroy my own body. The concept was fascinating, and this cancer cell had not just survived but had thrived and multiplied to the state where it had now taken over my kidney, and if nothing was done, it would certainly have taken over the host body, which would be me.

I thought that even this successful compromising of my normal cells with the cancer cells was truly amazing, that the end result would eliminate any chance for the cancerous continuation of life, so any success is doomed for failure, for if the cancer were to succeed, it would kill me. What complicated and absorbing flood of thoughts had taken over my mind. A brief few weeks ago, I had given little thought to cancer, and now it was the sole object of my scrutiny and conscious thoughts. I was a prisoner in body to this disease, and if I let it, I would be a prisoner in spirit as well.

I felt in a way that cells from my body, even mutated cancer oncogenes, were a part of me, and how ironic that parts of me were on a mission of survival, which would inevitably become a death mission. My own death squad was out to destroy me by fighting for their survival. I couldn't think of any kind of symbiotic relationship that both parties are destroyed at the end. This was truly a complicated revelation that I rolled around inside me for quite some time.

We dismiss thoughts and ideas, bad thoughts and dark imaginings removed easily, and wonderful pleasing thoughts regretfully fall as well. Memories fade and dreams subside. Goals, once so attainable, fall from reach. The time we're given seems never enough. Time that lingers, perhaps providing reason, and time that flees, taking with it a cure.

The child we were is no longer here. The little baby has grown and shed its features, replaced over and over by newer versions of ourselves until replication ceases to function, and the telomeres on our cells no longer permit cellular replacement.

Eventually I figured out that there are so many pieces of ourselves that we render useless and discard, that it was okay to think of the cancer cells as enemies, out to hurt us. I thought about infections we get, where great amounts of mucous and puss are produced, yet we don't harbor any attachments or worry that it's a part of us. I thought about waste removal on a cellular level, cell regeneration, and all the pieces of our bodies that are constantly being replicated and replaced daily, resulting in almost a whole body being replicated, repeatedly throughout our lifetime.

Incessantly we are disposing of pieces of our very existence. Knowingly or not the process continues till the body stops the balancing act, when homeostasis and respiration, can no longer produce desirable results. Death on a cellular plane, apoptosis, is pre-programed and designed to eradicate the genetic mutations from conquering the normal replication process, yet this too can falter and allow cancer to multiply with impunity.

At some point a realization that we are what we eat, and physician heal thyself, came over me, and I knew that I was to blame for my body's invasion of my normalcy, and that I would be mostly if not completely responsible for the curing, the managing, and the acceptance of my life at this point and at every further moment of my limited time on this planet. How could I ever consider that I was alone or without precedent in the fight against an internal invasion by my body toward my body? I realized life itself was the gift I had long ignored, and that even now I was receiving such amazing gifts. My incidental finding of my cancer during a botched biopsy, without which I probably would have died by now, is a gift enjoyed daily. I doubt much that the gift of life itself was ever more appreciated than by someone who was snatched back from death's door, or who was given a medical death sentence, but still wakes each day to sunrises, smiles, and perhaps a fresh cup of coffee.

CHAPTER 9

"PLEASE STOP, I WON'T DO IT NO MORE"

Whenever somebody relates some self-perceived terrible incident in their lives, something that happened on the way to work, like they missed the bus, had a flat tire, or got pulled over for a traffic ticket, I listen for the point when after all the complaining, they say something like "You wouldn't believe it." I marvel at what some people find a bad experience, and then I agree with them and add to the dialogue about how wrong it was to leave the lid up, on the toilet, the lid off on the ketchup, and wished they'd put a lid on themselves.

I walked into the oncologist's waiting room with my brother, also a cancer survivor, for the first time, and said to all the people in the NYC office, "Hi, I guess you all got cancer or you'd be somewhere else," "Anywhere else," "We're from Jersey," and "We have cancer too." "Okay, you can all go back to staring at the walls now." "Boy this is sure one tough crowd." "Anybody here know any good cancer jokes?"

I paused and explained that my attempt at humor was not due to some childhood trauma, like when I was thrown into a closet in kindergarten for crying or any head injury back in the fifth grade, due to the neighborhood kids placing rocks in the snowballs, when we were "growing up." I further assured all present that my behavior in the oncology waiting room of a prestigious NYC hospital most certainly had absolutely nothing to do with the technicians scolding

73

me outside the CT scan room of my hospital in Jersey for using the word *cancer* in their hospital, and that they don't use that word there. Everyone seemed as excited about my explanation for my introduction, as they were about the introduction.

It seemed to me that the best way to conquer fear is with some other emotion; any other emotion will suffice, and for me attempts at humor, whether humorous or not, do the trick, and chase the fear from many topics and life situations. Thus, my entrance into most doctors' offices brings about an outpouring of emotions followed by an unusual degree of concern from most patients and all medical personnel.

Neglectful desk receptionists I greet with loud coughing and words shouted out as if I was unable to hear, seems to get their attention immediately. The obligatory questionnaire on initial visit can be easily dismissed by informing them that you either you don't have your glasses with you and can't see, or the glasses you have on are not yours, the wrong prescription, an old pair; thus once again, you can't see enough to fill the forms.

Loud patients can be silenced by being louder and even more obnoxious. It won't win friends, but it usually shuts them up. Cell phone blabbermouths can be ridiculed into silence by fake talking into a cupped hand over your ear, repeating whatever you hear them say with additional commentary about how rude it is of the person next to you to be blabbing on the phone. When you take your hand away from your ear and show you have no phone, you can count on quite a few patients being jealous of how clever and creative you are, and some ... well, some people you wouldn't want for friends anyway.

Well, basically that's my story, and I'm sticking to it. I have been lucky enough to have survived without any intrusive chemo radiation or other therapies. I can't attribute it to anything in particular, but I do think my wonderful wife and mother have made the survival possible, and having a reason to live is a basic need in order to live.

I don't know if anybody else has had such adventures in the medical world, but I thought it almost my duty to record these things for posterity, and everybody I told my stories to laughed. Some cried, but most laughed. I close these memoirs with the notation that I have been blessed with the ability to continue life for nine years and counting. Looks like the five-year survival rate was less a limit than a reachable goal to surpass. I wish the best of luck to all who suffer the scourge of cancer and especially to those who love us.

CHAPTER 10

AND THEN THERE WAS SANDY

A storm, a hurricane, a force unfamiliar in these parts, slammed into us on the last week of October 2012. All the weather forecasters earned their paychecks with this one, predicting the storm of a century, and we got the storm of the century. Death and destruction were part of life from the Jersey shore to Maine, millions upon millions of people without power light or heat.

At first awareness of the event taking shape around me, I viewed it as just another phony alert as we often hear, and there was just a slight amount of rain falling, despite predictions to the contrary. As I sat with the window open, I thought there wasn't enough wind to blow out a candle. So I drifted off to sleep, woke up in time to go to work, and no sooner had I gotten out of bed, headed for the bathroom, when the lights went out, and they stayed out for nine days.

In the beginning it was just a slight inconvenience. There was still cold food in the fridge and cold drinks, and we had a battery-operated radio. It seemed like no TV and news was the primary concern, not to mention we couldn't see anything in the darkness. I went to work.

No streetlights, no traffic lights, and after a very harrowing trip, I made it to work. I called my wife on the cell phone, which was nearly dead and no means to charge it up. Things were looking worse. At work we have generators, and lights were on everywhere, seemed like being at work was the best place to be—nah.

As the darkness prevailed with no predictions of power being returned in anytime soon, we started to try and gather some basic essentials for surviving the next few days and maybe weeks. Flashlights were gone from the shelves as were all sizes of batteries. ATM machines were without power, so money was no longer a moment away. Gas stations either had no gas or no power to pump it out of the ground.

One day as I was going to work, I saw a line of cars outside a gas station, and another long line of people with gas cans. It didn't dawn on me right away that it was people getting gas for their generators. I switched my search from batteries to finding a generator, and drove to store after store, without any being for sale. I had to balance my need for gas and my desire for generator power. I found a gas station with no lines (yet) and filled up and went all the way to a Home Depot in New York State. I cruised the NY throughway until I saw a great big shopping area off the throughway. I pulled in front of the store, and in the window was a freshly painted sign that read NO GENERATORS. I drove home disappointed and out of gas and patience.

After a few days, huge gas lines started to appear on the highways, and in town the lines weaved around blocks and took up entire lanes of main streets. After a while, police officers were at them to control tempers and people's natural affinity to cut in line. We waited in one long line for nearly two hours, with people cutting in line and shouting at each other. When we got a few cars away from the gas pumps, the attendants started waving their arms and running their hands across their necks shouting "No gas. No gas."

We regrouped, shrugged off the disappointment, thought about others that lost life and property, and moved on in search of gasoline, like pioneers we were on the trail seeking our fortune. At least on the road we had music, news, and heat and got out of the rustic candlelit cabin, which was now our home.

We finally found another line that didn't seem as long as other lines and pulled in for the wait for service. Approaching our turn at the pump, we were apprehensive if we would really be finally getting gas this time.

I pulled up to the pump after an hour or more being in line and pulled out my credit card and said, "Fill it up."

"No credit cards," the man said without looking up from what he was doing. I looked in my wallet saw I had $80, four twenty dollar bills, so I said, "No problem, fill it up."

When the pump shut off at $69, I handed him the four twenties, waiting for change, and he said, "No change," and he walked off to the next victim.

I complained to another attendant that looked like the owner, and he said, "Hell we all gotta make a living."

"Yeah," I said, "but we don't have to rip each other off during this crisis."

The price per gallon was about fifty cents more than nearby stations. Incredible how a miserable feeling can come from just getting some gas.

We finally were able after three days to get enough candles and a propane lantern to light the apartment. We had access to an ATM machine on our block. The good people of Chase had rented an industrial towed-in generator, so we all had money, except there were lines for that privilege as well. Plus, we had our radio, which reminded me of the old pictures of people listening to the radio before TV was invented. They would look at it to listen. I found myself doing the same thing.

Conservation of resources seemed to be the primary objective during this crisis, and we had a candle in each room that you could light if needed. We had purchased enough propane that I would leave the light on low in the kitchen. What seems now like such a little thing was a great spirit lifter, to have that light on and be able to turn it up on high and illuminate the whole room. Food preparation and eating was best done during the day to save on candles and batteries. Washing was limited to heating water on a two-burner Coleman stove, and not too efficient a process it remained during the entire nine days.

After two or three days, you start to believe this may not end too soon, and you start to think of ways to do things that don't require batteries and power and new ways to do old things. It took three days and miles and miles of driving to finally find ice. Yes, ice. It made me think of the days before refrigeration when ice was cut in the winter, smack out of the frozen lakes. Then it was stored in a warehouse to use as the seasons go by.

Three days just to find ice. We went to five Wal-Marts and every supermarket we came across while driving from town to town. Small corner stores and bodegas had no power, so no ice, and most had the doors open for selling nonperishable items for cash. If we weren't so desperate for ice, it would have been a lovely quaint ride through the towns reminiscent of days gone by, with people out on the street actually talking with each other. Seems like in a crisis most people revert to their better beings, and shed the clothing of hatred and distrust that has become so comfortable, but that's just my opinion.

We pulled into our local supermarket at my wife's insistence even though I saw the lights were out, so how could there be any ice, I thought. Even a simple task as this was further complicated by the lack of traffic signals and police officers directing most motorists out of town to keep their jurisdictions well ordered. It seemed like a good idea, but I had to drive several miles in the wrong direction before I could make a U-turn and head back in the right direction. Simplicity had disappeared as well during this crisis as every simple thing was now a complex of hurdles and mazes. B didn't follow A anymore, and I was the worse for wear over it. Frustration was easily had by any who braved this new world order of things, and it was only day three.

We eventually pull into the Shoprite, and we see the lights are on, and people are buying stuff and paying at the cash registers—hooray for normalcy. I quickly commandeer a motorized handicapped shopping cart and proceed to the back of the store where I know they have the cooler for ice. As soon as I arrive, there was a worker with a load of ice on a pallet jack that he was about to load in the freezer. There were about twenty bundles of ice with six bags inside each bundle. He looked at me as I was raising my arms to heaven to thank God for so much ice, and asked me how many I wanted. I told him to throw a whole bundle in the small basket in front of the cart I was driving. I backed up my cart and sat there as I watched in minutes how this entire skid of ice was devoured by customers that were in the right place at the right time. I proudly drove away in search of my wife who was somewhere in the store so I can show her my bounty.

Like the hunter home from the hills with the day's catch, I felt reprieved from the desolation of this new existence where each morsel is a battle against an enemy yet encountered. I carefully loaded the ice in my vehicle, mindful of others that would take what's mine in a moment if given half a chance. I felt more of a kinship with my ancient predecessors than I did with those around me. How true, I imagined, was the saying only the strong survived. How wrong and unfortunate, I sensed, it must have been in eons ago when knowledge or creative minds fell victim to the sword. Who be the judge of which individual possess the mightier skill. It all depended on the time, and now was the time for basic instinct and survival. Education and word skills would hardly get you any further than a broad back and strong arms, a throwback again, I noticed, to days gone by.

I drove by slowly with my cart and its precious cargo in front of the checkout lines gazing at all the people waiting to pay for their groceries along with their bag or two of ice. One lady had a sack of ice like I had procured, so I decided to speak with her. She said she "had driven all the way from Mahwah, NJ (about40miles), looking for ice and had given up." She pulled in this store and was turning around to go home, and she decided to give it "one more shot." Amazing how such common items can achieve treasure status due solely to their availability. I wondered what item would next become so valuable due to its scarcity, and would I be able to obtain it.

We had two coolers on the fire escape, which became our refrigerator and pantry du jour. Ice would stay ice for maybe three days, providing one cooler was just for food and the other was to get ice for cold drinks. Worse thing about this setup was when you opened the window to get what you wanted your heat escaped from the apartment and not least of all you could see just barely 150 feet away up the next block. The porch lights were on for that house and that block. I kept wishing the damn bulb would burn out so I wouldn't be reminded that next door all was indeed normal, and it was all just a matter of location, location, location.

Driving anywhere was the number one problem. The inescapable road trip was necessary and dreaded due to lights out, trees down, other motorists, pedestrians, and police officers, in each town. East Rutherford had power lines down, and police officers redirecting you to side streets that were flooded with residents standing on front steps in front of their street, which was now a lake. Carlstadt, Moonachie, and Little Ferry were all suffering from flooding just about anywhere you tried to go.

You would drive a bit then get stopped by other vehicles that weren't going to attempt crossing the newly developed lake. You would drive a ways and find it blocked by trees lying about with neighbors cutting some for firewood and just to get access to the street from their homes. You would drive a ways and find the roads blocked, and you would get detoured to some area you were never in before, so you were kind of lost in a place that normally doesn't look like it does now and won't look this way in the future.

Jersey City mostly had barricades set up to keep traffic out of the city. Good idea since most traffic is from people passing through to NYC or other areas, and all they do is make getting around town more difficult than it already was. Problem was they didn't make special exceptions because you live there. Coming home from work each morning and instead of traveling the shortest route home I would be redirected to whatever streets the police thought best, and I would travel nearly to Bayonne before I would find a spot where unseen I would make a U-turn and head back in at least the same direction before being sent on another tangent by one officer, some trines a lady cop directing traffic behind barricades.

It somewhat reminded me of 911 when the whole city was on lockdown and literally every major intersection and traffic light had officers with automatic weapons and body armor. They were doing their jobs, and we just had to make do with the inconveniences as best we could.

At nighttime we would look up and down the block and saw nothing but blackness. The swinging of flashlights as some people were out doing what they had to do, negotiating the darkness. The lack of any traffic signal seemed like there would be an accident every minute when the cars went by. Seemed to me that the only time to really do anything with safety was in the daylight hours, and the coming of night was like a signal to cease activity till the morning light, night being but a great closing of the day.

I imagined ancient times and what fears and difficulties each nighttime presented. Fear of what's out there, the sounds but not being able to see anything. I also thought of how many countless generations had to survive without all the things we have that we only miss in times like these. No easy way to get light or a fire for warmth or to see at night. No refrigeration and all the food that was eaten that today we would quickly throw out. Medical emergencies and other work required at night so difficult, and now we were living with the same limited capacity for life, except we knew there was a better and safer way to live than our ancestors during their struggle to survive.

On the third day, or maybe the fourth, we decided to empty the contents of the refrigerator. It's amazing how much stuff winds up in there, so many opened and half-used items.

At first we tried to determine what was still good, what was definitely bad, and what was maybe okay to eat right away. I had kept some ice in there, and we tried not to open it at all, wishing the power would soon come back on and everything could possibly be saved. Well, fungi and bacteria are not concerned with any monetary concerns, nor do they share my need for unspoiled food stuffs, so as you can imagine, we filled several trash bags with what was up into yesterday called food but had to be renamed garbage today. Everything went out—milk, eggs, meats, frozen meat, frozen vegetables frozen anything, frozen everything, pot pies, steaks, hamburgers, and all the condiments associated with them—ketchup, mustard, sauces, fruits.

Our basic routine consisted of monitoring the radio for any clues as to when it would be over and obtaining food at amounts equal to or less than needed for a single day. Of course, this adjustment to manage food stuffs had a negative impact on gas usage, and our truck used a lot of gas. I suppose the value of an object is based upon how much you want it and how hard it is to get, but to me it always seemed ice was my most desired commodity. We found out later in the week that the gov was giving out free ice at various locations. We finally tracked a place down and acquired several super-large bags of ice that contained cubes all melted together. Too awkward and messy and inconvenient, so we went back to searching and buying what we could when we could.

We had an automotive jump starter that had outlets for 110v, so I brought it in the house for some emergency electricity. We were undecided at first whether to watch TV or cook a pizza. Sadly, we decided that we wanted to microwave a frozen pizza we knew was in the freezer, and if it wasn't cooked real soon, it would become unusable. We plugged in the microwave and the charger started hissing and smoking, making strange sounds until it died. Fingers crossed we checked the microwave and found mush inside the oven. Oh well, you never know.

Undefeated and determined to satisfy at least one yearning during the crisis—sort of to let nature know we can take it, we are modern men and we can deal with a storm, hurricane, or whatever they were calling it of the century—we headed for the bar down the street. Yes, the bar. It had a generator, the place was lit, and they had cold drinks and best of all a television. We watched a benefit concert with Bruce Springsteen, and we decided to buy a TV to run on batteries. We couldn't find a TV that ran on batteries or one that would operate with 12 volts, so we bought one anyway along with an inverter. We also needed to buy a special antenna for decent reception. It wouldn't work in the house since we fried the charger, so we would go out to the car, plug in the inverter plug in the TV, and sit and watch.

It wasn't so much the quality of the shows on the television but the fact that we had found the ability to amuse or distract ourselves from the drudgery of living like a homeless family since home was barely livable, and we had somehow outsmarted the forces that were keeping us in the dark. For the remainder of the power outage, we would go outside as soon as we ate some food and set up the TV on the dashboard, situate the very large antenna against the sunroof, plug everything in, and bring something to drink, some ice, some blankets, and enjoy anything that came on. The colors and clarity were fabulous. We would fall asleep in the car watching sports or a movie or the news. It was very special.

The special feelings felt were due to being together under stressful situation and being comfortable after all. It was pitch-black outside. After an hour or two into the darkness, vehicles were rare except for the ever-present patrol cars cruising up down and around town, which was absolutely a welcome sight. People would walk by and stop and stare in to see what we were doing in there. They would smile and shake their heads in acknowledgment of what a great idea to be in the car being able to watch television.

It truly was a lot of fun to see people strain to see what we were watching. At one point I thought that the television would draw a crowd and become bothersome, but that never happened.

We had to start the truck up every hour or so to avoid a dead battery and to get heat. So it was a trade-off, enjoy myself with my wife doing what few others could do alone and wait in line for hours to get more gas. It was no contest. Enjoying each other's company feeling like in a lifeboat surviving after a shipwreck, thinking of so many walking about unable to sleep in their homes. We had definitely found and created a cozy habitat to wait out the return to normalcy that was just a few more days away. Plus, we felt some semblance of control was restored after so much we take for granted had simply vanished from our lives. I hope others fared as well.

RAP
Jersey City NJ 2012

CHAPTER 11

9/11/04

Three years ago, the tragedy that became known as 9/11 was thrust upon the shores of this great land, three years ago our lives were forever changed.

Death, horror, and disbelief, filled our hearts and souls, as the Twin Towers sank before a nation's eyes.

I watched the towering plumes of smoke, rising from the canyons of Manhattan I watched as the once glistening shafts of steel and glass plummeted from my sight. Dreamlike, in disbelief, I tried to rationalize what my eyes had seen and my heart had felt.

Cries of shock and fear echoed from the gathered citizens that had amassed along the waterfront. Unable to accept or believe what we had just seen, we looked for someone to wake us from this nightmare. Unable to believe the Twin Towers, once so tall and prominent, were in seconds ... gone from the skyline.

Unable to believe, that the billowing clouds of smoke were all that we could see. Only able to feel the tragedy that had been thrust upon us, the immensity of it all, the loss of so many lives in an instant. The sudden and complete realization that all that once was, could never be again, and what would happen next.

Like a magnet, I am drawn to this place, that three years and a day ago was just a nice place to view the New York skyline, but has now become almost a surrealistic reminder of the hate for this great land. A festering hatred has resulted in this ultimate loss of life, and innocence, leaving forever, a sense of fear and doubt, about our own safety, our own lives, and our freedom.

Unable to accept or believe what we had just seen, we looked for someone or something to wake us from this nightmare. Weeks will go by and the smoke would still rise from Lower Manhattan. It seemed as though the flaming inferno would forever burn, and nothing could extinguish it, or the pain that only intensifies with every conscious thought of that day.

Three years ago I took everything for granted … the alarm goes off, the lights come on with a flick of a switch … the stove lights, and the bacon sizzles. The shower is warm and the clothes are clean. The car starts and I kiss my wife goodbye. I tell her I love her and she says to be careful.

The radio announcer gives the traffic report, and I merge into the inevitable traffic. And all of this I took for granted, when in the time it takes to read these words, it can all be taken away. Nine eleven did not cause this reality; it just made the reality more aware to us. Saying our farewells when we part for the day can literally become our last words. Tragically and regrettably this is the way of the world today.

I sit here at the water's edge … people have gathered, lags are in place flowers are in abundance, the blue sky is speckled with white clouds, birds are flying through the air and boats sail up the Hudson River. But something else is here, the overwhelming sense of loss, the realization of how swift our lives can be taken. The sense of how brief our time and how vulnerable and unpredictable is our existence.

Sunlight flickers off the crests of tiny waves as they ripple across the river then disappear on the shoreline, like so many bright lives … gone in an instant that has become forever.

Pleasure boats now fill the harbor, but helicopters also are here, a police presence covers the streets … a constant reminder that serenity can suddenly become discord and the unimaginable can become reality.

Three years ago the sunshine was blocked by the thick black smoke of thousands of gallons of aviation fuel, and the burning steel and glass of the once mighty towers. Day became night, hope became fear, and what couldn't be … was. Two thousand five hundred and eighty-nine lives, gone in an instant hundreds of thousands of loved ones, thrust into instant agony. Nothing will ever be the same, and nothing has ever been the same since.

More lives were lost at the towers than were lost at Pearl Harbor. Three years ago, I was a much different person, but so were all of us.

9/11/15

So much time has passed since that awful day, yet the frightening memories are today as vivid as ever. We live now in a different world, where enhanced security is everywhere, from the airport screenings and government buildings screening, to a police presence at any construction work being done.

The reality of the ever-present danger grows daily as we are witness to countless disgraceful and inhuman beheadings and bombings and murdering of countless innocent human beings in all corners of the globe.

The chants of these fanatics is death to all who do not conform to their religious beliefs, which at first glance seems unique and new, but history reveals an endless succession of religions who preach their dogma and murder and slaughter in the name of their God.

I do not believe God (my personal belief) or the majority of others' interpretations and belief, have given in to any perception of God, telling them to kill others that believe or worship in a different means. The proposition that God is one side or another seems rather ungodlike to me and sort of a confusion of their reality and beliefs. The massive wasting of human life is proof of the insanity of these groups who daily conspire to end our way of life and our very life's themselves.

We have countless government organizations and individuals that daily speak out against such atrocities, but little actually stops these determined less-than-human fanatics. We live our lives with the awareness of such a reality, and 9/11 has brought that awareness into our everyday way of life.

It is an undeniable and unchangeable fact that we have to live with this awful memory, but if we ever forget that day, and it is possible to actually forget or deny the event, just look at how some people believe there was no such event as the Holocaust. If we do, we are doomed to repeat it.

The 9/11 Memorial at ground zero has been for me an over-whelming experience of emotions. You could feel that something happened here. You can feel the agony of those who suffered and died there, and mixed with the video coverage of that day's tragedy, and the eyewitness descriptions of such unspeakable events, it becomes a surrealistic experience for the body and heart.

But to visit this site is a testament to the human spirit, to lift oneself up by their bootstrap, to continue on with our lives and show those responsible that we are not defeated, we have not been destroyed, and to show them that we are Americans.

9/11/16

I have always felt a close spiritual connection to the tragedy we know as 911 ever since I saw the second tower disappear before my eyes. The image has become permanent as is the endless billowing clouds of smoke from ground zero that lasted for months.

Every year me and my wife Corina would go down to the memorial service that Jersey City put on. Every year we cried as the bagpipes played and the flag hung from the fire department hook and ladders swayed in the constant breeze at Exchange Place, the same breeze that blew the smoke over and turned daytime into night so many years ago.

Since last I wrote about this tragedy of epic size, I have also suffered beyond belief. I have lost my mother, my father, and my wife. The ability not to focus on anything but that loss is now something I share with the thousands, the hundreds of thousands, who lost their loved ones that day. We are left to wonder and grieve about how such things can be in our world. My wife died suddenly and without warning, so there exists a feeling of kinship with those on 911 that suddenly without warning had their loved ones taken from our hearts.

I struggle to understand how I could have lost my parents and my wife so suddenly, as I live through this anniversary of sudden and tragic loss and I realize the amount of suffering that one event caused to decent, blameless people. No answers are forthcoming to these thoughts besides a realization that there exists in this world a radical hatred some have, for our country, and their unholy pursuit to achieve their goals with such vicious, dastardly deeds.

As the nation once more mourns of this tragedy, we are reminded weekly of the terrorism that dominates the peace we would choose for this world. We remain stunned that such political beliefs and dogma result in such cowardly acts upon the innocent, to protest perceived acts, alleged actions by the not so innocent. Nothing could ever explain. No words bear any semblance of connotation to satisfy the why, to somehow explain the attack against America and the world. The objections of the conduct and actions of our nation should not be remedied by the random executions of innocent citizenry. But rational judgment takes a back seat to wanton terrorism.

How certain then becomes the uncertainty of life. Without control or input for a desired outcome, we are but spectators, witness to the intolerable, the unimaginable, the very worst that humans can do to each other. The unthinkable can quickly without forewarning become the unbearable. Now I too must bear that burden, having done nothing to cause the suffering that will be my constant companion until I too part from this earth.

While these acts, which unquestionably stem from pure hate, cloaked in some unbelievable religious garb, the hatred that caused it does not spread its venom to the innocent. We do not desire to kill the innocent of some other religious tribe; we do not vocalize hate toward the religion that these hoodlums came from. Evilness and the evil exist in all corners of the globe. Hatred, it seems, is an easier way to go through life for some than peaceful coexistence. All one has to do is look at Israel to see the ridiculousness and height of hatred that man can somehow lower himself into.

I have suffered more than I thought I would ever have to in this life, and every day, every moment, is truly a battle to choose life and to continue being a kind, decent human worthy of my Maker's intent. So I live each day each moment with faith and love, and I will never succumb to the evilness that others so quickly embrace.

God bless,
Apple

CHAPTER 12

KNOW NOTHINGS

Well, it's finally out, the truth be known, 90 percent—which is about as close to all of everything as you can get, 90 percent of the known. Detectable, visible with our technological advanced infrared, radio, and wide-field array telescope systems have led scientists to the inescapable conjecture that 90 percent of all that there is in the Universe is unknown. All the planets, and galaxies, nebulas and star clusters that we see equal about 10 percent of what exists; the other 90 percent, we know nothing about.

They call it dark matter and dark energy, and virtually nothing is known, no physical properties, no chemical signature, no visible or invisible rays of energy, nothing, and it makes up 90 percent of the universe. All the centuries of accumulated scientific discoveries, experiments, explorations, and observations add up to a mere 10 percent. It's as if we know our own hands, but not what they're connected to, or what the rest of the body looks like or how it functions.

How in God's name did we come to this revelation, after so much funded research into our solar system, and our place in the universe, however small that first appeared to be. Now it turns out we know a lot less proportionally than an ant in the jungle might know of the jungle, with its myriad plant and animal life. How curious then is the attitude that we are the masters of our destiny and the shapers of our future, when we are neither, and in fact we don't even have a clue to what this is, and how we got here.

Turns out our limited vision is more limited than anyone had thought. Our knowledge of things that are, is infinitesimal. Well, it makes all the geniuses less far away in their reported understanding of things we can't understand. Should make us feel a little better that the know-it-alls actually know very little.

As for me, I have always felt that the more I learned about something, anything, the more it made me question, and thus revealed to me how much less I really knew. You see a car. You find out it's called a certain name. You find out what kind of horsepower and gas mileage it gets. You find out the bore and stroke of the engine, the number of camshafts. Further questioning reveals the engine block is made of an aluminum alloy. You find out how aluminum is smelted from ore dug up in a mine and made into ingots for industry.

Further involvement leads to molecular structure of aluminum and the periodic table of elements, leading us to discover that the elements us and the car are made of come from the earth, which come from star collisions or explosions eons ago that spread the material across galaxies, to be reformed in the planets and stars we see today. And then we have the dark matter and dark energy that nobody knows anything about besides that it exists. What fantastic scientific frontiers lay ahead, what immense discoveries await the future scientist and explorers? We are on the cusp of new knowledge that may make all other knowledge obsolete or at least trivial.

I can't imagine some grade school child saying that everything has already been discovered there's nothing left to find when the complete opposite is true. Like the blind man that feels the trunk of an elephant and claims to the world that an elephant is much like a snake. Limited input reveals limited results. Fantastic, new technologies have to be discovered or invented, as we travel this journey to discovery. We are like babes in the woods, children amongst the stars. We are on more of an exciting journey that even Carl Sagan could have predicted.

These revelations are not limited to the vastness of "outer space" or the "cosmos." No, these discoveries pertain to the smaller scale of our discoveries, the atomic world. The vast distances between the nucleus and the orbiting electron, not unlike the earth orbiting the sun, is filled with dark matter. The smaller we delve into particle physics, the more the distances reveal themselves, and we are just now discovering that even these tiniest of tiny worlds are 90 percent dark matter and dark energy. It's like waking up in a movie theater, and you slept through most of the movie and now they're showing you the big ending, except it is the great beginning.

For me from a scientific point of view, I believe the more and more we discover about our existence, the deeper we unveil each peel or layer to expose yet again new discoveries. It means just one thing, that God has created so vast a creation, it can never be completely understood, and that it remains folly for man to persist and persevere in his quest for discovering some origins or a fuller understanding of what how and the why of anything. I see God in the smallest of places when scientists talk of parts that make up the smallest part of a proton or neutron, the quark particles that haves aspects or characteristics referred to as charm up and down and so on.

In the world of the very large where the nearest galaxy is a million light years away, with light itself being used as a measuring stick for such vast distances, I also see the hand of God. Space is or isn't curved, the existence of black holes, dying suns where everything gets sucked into it including light. Matter and antimatter, Nebulae where stars are born, billions of galaxies in the vastness of space and time. Time for us we measure correlated to our own life expectancy of less than one hundred years, to billions of years of planets or stars coming into existence, running their course and fading into obscurity with a bang or shrinking into the heavens or lighting up skies where no human eyes can testify to.

Why it took so long for the scientist to admit they really know nothing about anything is understandable, what doctor will tell you he knows nothing about the body or cancer, when the truth is, after all their studying and service they still have little knowledge of how and why the body functions as it does. Once again the hand of God can be seen as you learn about the incredible thing your body does millions of times a day without your knowledge or even your input. I know of only some of the systems, and when you learn of all the things going on at a cellular or a blood level, you develop questions that can't be answered, like how does the body know to do these things, what switches cells on or off, why do we age, or even why do we die?

Basically the point of all this for me is that wherever you look deep enough, or long enough at something, big small or introspective, I come to the same conclusion each and every time. I see the product of God, I see the results of God, and I see everywhere proof of his creation. Deeper and deeper or farther out in space, it is as clear as can be. I don't know why or for what reason all this is here, but I believe there is no *end*, no final destination of discovery on the small or the large scale. I think also that these scientific discoveries were maybe put there for us to discover. As a child discovers his world little by little, perhaps we as humans discover ours little by little.

I hope that our waning interest doesn't fade before our discoveries pan out. I can't believe that all the intricacies involved in life, form big to small, are not there to be discovered. I find it impossible to accept, that all these systems evolved by themselves, that our brain just evolved over time form an assemblage of cells. I do not think what we are, and what we see today, were not imagined at some previous point. Before time perhaps?

I
I want …
Nights filled with silence, and days soaked with sunshine
I want the beauty of a sunset, to spark new awakenings
The crispness of the morning dew, to drip with the yearning for
    freedom
I want kindness to be everywhere, and fear to be not

I want …
The sounds of children playing, to satiate my ears, and gladden my
    heart
I want tears abolished from memory, replaced with children's laughter
With merriment and happiness served up as the main course
I want hope to be the choice, the only choice

ONE HELL OF A TOOTHACHE

I want ...
Church bells to ring out, dogs to bark, and people to cheer
I want Love to surround each of us till we are called away from here
Love to heal, to cure, to support, to lean on, to give and to receive
I want Love so pure, given freely, without expected reciprocation to
    burst upon us all

I want ...
The sweetness of tender moments to be engrained upon our soul
I want each and every second of life to be free of pain and suffering
To be adorned with beauty and fulfillment of a heart's desire
I want nothing more than everything

I want ...
Peace and understanding, or its equivalent, to be the first goal
    between people
I want war, violence, hatred and humiliation to be stripped of any
    legitimacy
And thrown upon the dung heap with racism, bigotry, and brutality
I want each soul to be able to rise to their full potential

I want ...
Simplicity and uncomplicated ideas to flood the world with saving
    ways
I want Mother Earth to be free of the ugliness we as humans have
    brought to her
And allow the seas to heal and the fauna and flora to share life on
    our planet
I want random acts of kindness to be more than just random, but
    habitual

I want ...
The remainder of life to be reflected by the cool breeze of the ocean
    water
I want the glorious ocean to overwhelm my senses with echoes from
    the past

As the surf removes and replenishes in each pass from sea to shore
I want my life to be as new as the sea and as old as the sea, nothing
being wasted

I want …
The irrevocable sanity we were all given to guide us through to the
next generation
I want to pass on something more than burden and shame for our
selfishness
Something as simple as hope as rare as wisdom and as missing as
charity
I want life to be as precious as it always has been to be as precious in
the future

I want …
Our children's children to be given a chance for greatness as was
given to us
I want the bearers of the future to embrace each challenge and soar
to unimaginable heights
To reach plateaus we never dreamed possible, how wonderful that
would truly be, my God think of it
I want perhaps too much, but if moral capability has been passed, the
goals are just a matter of distance

CHAPTER 13

CORINA

How easy the days were with you at my side. So easy came a smile. Laughter flowed as easy as a mountain creek toward the river. Life from within was seamless and without fears. Days and nights at your side streamed effortlessly toward a future sought with anxious hope. Years followed with a comfort and familiarity that few get to experience.

Seldom taken each other for granted, and always happy to receive outward expressions of our love and desire, we left the early awkwardness couples sometimes feel, and became as one. Knowing each other it seemed better than we knew ourselves, predicting before actual thoughts one another's reactions and moods.

A comfort beyond words or explanation, a relationship understood only by those who have been blessed enough to share one. Existing and exploring a sense of membership with the human family beyond birth or bloodlines.

A commonality we shared, with lovers across the ages that have lived and loved without fear or regard to society's rules and norms. Gentleness and kindness filled our lives, leaving no room for discord or tribulation, at peace with the world and in love with each other.

An inner light and glow seemed to nurture and enrich our lives. From the simplest of daily events to soul-searching depths of life-threatening medical or freedom issues, there was an undeniable confidence in the support by each other for each other.

Impenetrable was our alliance, unbreakable by evil thoughts actions or deeds. Only death in the end forced us physically from each other.

Now the time spent with my Corina are at the core of every action and thought, her beauty and wisdom fill my eyes and heart every moment I breathe. Her witty remarks and sayings flow from my mouth as if they were mine, and they are. Corina is as much me as I am her, and till the last exhale I make upon this earth, it will have her in it as she always will be in my soul.

I walk upon this gentle ground and see things different since she left. Sunsets are not as exciting, and sudden sun showers don't thrill me anymore. Bare minimum of thought goes into any new idea that she was not party to. Passing of time is just an action without any offering on my part to infuse anything of value.

Some say I am getting better, but they speak from kindness not experience, I think, and I have gotten different for sure, but never will I be better since the best part of me and of my life experience has ceased to exist in this world.

Colors of the spectrum exchanging places vying for view, yet we go on with our lives sometimes without notice of our own beauty in the scheme of life. Some people come into or lives like a bright sunlight and illuminate our darkness making us complete. We try as best we can to hold on to that person, but not unlike the brightness of a noonday sun, their light will fade into reds and oranges and return back to wherever it is we come from. I wish so much to have made that journey together, but like the power I have over a sunset, I find it impossible to change one instant of vibrancy or enchantment that my Corina has given to me. Without doubt she was the best that ever happened in my life, my very own sun and sunlight, but her passing is the worst that could ever happen, and the coldness of life without her warmth, her love, and her sunshine shall darken my journey till the end of time.

I don't know if I will ever know why I or any of us grieve, for they are still alive in our hearts and thought of daily. But to not hold and hug and smile with her, just the thought rips through me like a hurricane, leaving me wet from the flood of tears and exhausted for pleading out loud for some reason for this loneliness and misery. Never when together did I ever give thought that we could be separated, and I would have to exist without my sole purpose for life. All the joy and happiness is but distant memories that crash into this new reality, leaving me weak and hurting. I know no cure or easy journey through, but time has changed me, and I am changed, not better, just different, not from choice or desire just a different soul, weakened and damaged.

> It's all the little things, ya know
> The loving things
> That hurt so much now, ya know
> To be without you
> Is to be without life, I know

I know that all life is change, and tomorrow is not guaranteed, but I am still knocked out cold from the death of my best friend and soulmate, my honey Corina. Minutes and hours turn into days and weeks, and now a whole year has passed with me on the planet, and Corina has never been more alive in my mind. I hear her and see her and feel her always.

I used to tell my honey that as long as you're thinking of someone they are kept alive. I always talked about my grandmother and my friend Frankie and how they were still alive in different thoughts and actions through the day that reminded me of them. I had endless stories about experiences we shared, and Corina always enjoyed my reminiscing. I have not been able to not think about her, the things we did, things we said and all life's adventures we experienced. *Together* is the word I would best use to describe us, always together, out of choice and desires. She was my best listener, and I was hers.

There were several people who used to admire our closeness and banter, which was how we always were. People on the street, stores, and all the doctors' offices we went to. When they saw us coming, their face lit up because they knew somehow we were gonna make their day a little brighter.

Whether I sit the whole weekend in our apartment or drive to the ends of the Earth in search of some alternate reality, it never seems to help with what my doctors, psychiatrists, and bon vivants call grief attacks. No conscious effort or mechanical alteration of scenery or habitat has yet to allow my brain to resist the all-consuming realization of loss of everything I wanted and needed and loved.

I know I am very different than a year ago, not better, not worse, just different. Without Corina's daily input in my life, I drift off to places unknown, and without any maternal support or guidance or love and caring, the path seems dreary and without that spark of life that made every day and every hour special with my honey. I am not fearful of any outcome, either financial or medical, my only wish is for speed.

Time used to be so against us, never enough time to do anything, and now time is merely the moments that pass between what I see and what I don't any longer have, and awaiting any outcome but the current status I endure. To be separated from the one I love without possibility of any future connection is beyond comprehension by anyone, beyond any limit that the heart and soul can reach.

To have inside all the glorious and private events of our life together, all the thousands of little gentile kindnesses, and whispering of love, the sacrifices made for and with each other, to be eternally separated from her heart and soul is a fate worse than death. Something reserved for the wickedly evil, the tyrants that troll the earth throughout time immemorial.

Life without love for any caring, sentient being is but a farce, an impossible task beyond anything imaginable. We live and love sometimes without any visible effects of it, but once taking away the results are easily seen, and deeply felt. I remember always having a smile on my face, which would grow in proportion to my proximity to Corina. I remember and visualize always all the facial quirks and grimaces and signs she made to me throughout the day. Her character and personality had a propensity toward humor and laughter through thick and thin. I miss this so very much.

I suppose what will always be till I die is the loss of her personality and spirit toward life. She was an original, unafraid of anything, loving, kind, and filled with sunshine, and she was in love with me. In love with me, I can't believe I was so lucky she felt that way and so cursed to have lost my love of a lifetime, my dearest Corina.

Consider the honeybee ...

As it tirelessly works each day from plant to plant in its efforts to make honey. For its own survival it pollinates one-sixth of the world's fruits and vegetables.

Another benefit from these actions is to provide floral abundance to add to the majestic landscapes and floral beauty of our world and provide habitat for so many other insects and birds to flourish.

No wonder then that I always called my Corina Honey, as she provided my world with beauty and survival, by spreading her love and pollinating my thoughts and desires, enabling my life to be enriched and colorful and with meaning and purpose like that of the simple honeybee.

CHAPTER 14

CANNOT

I found that holding on to hatred or things that you know were wrong that somebody did only hurts yourself. I don't have hatred left in me. I got rid of it over time. Any recent botherings by others that do whatever they do sheds off me like rain on a tin roof. I bear no ill feelings toward anyone. I'm too drained from worrying about the future and health and where now to live, and like wow, everything has changed, but it's still just me here. I can't hold Corina's hand, and I can't get angry over it. I can't talk with Mom, and I can't get angry over it. I can't die in the house I was raised and worked on my whole life, and I can't get angry over it. I even found no problem paying for my biological father's cremation and urn. I can't get mad over anything others do, regardless of the pain and suffering they inflict upon me. I will bend and not break I am still here despite my desire not to be, and I can't get angry at that either.

... and lastly (end)

"So, Mr. Piombino, how long have you known you was crazy?"

"What?"

"I asked how long have you known that you were crazy."

"Oh, by long, what reference to the word *long* did you mean? If I might ask?"

"Timewise Mr. Piombino, timewise."

"I just wanted to narrow your request down. Okay, well, not too long."

"Again, Mr. Piombino, may we call you Robert?"

"How long in time was our request to you, will you comply with our request, please?"

"Certainly, which request do you mean?"

"All three."

"Yes, you may, don't know, and what again was the other one, I have a bad memory, ya know."

"Several times we have asked you how long have you known you were crazy."

"And what was my reply?"

"Fine, let's try this another way."

"Mr. Piombino, uhmm, I'm sorry, I mean, Robert, do you think you are normal?"

"Oh yes, most definitely, absolutely and may I add, positively, yes, I do."

"So based upon that answer, how do you explain your activities lately, or more specifically in the last year or so?"

"I can't explain, I can't understand, I can't."

"Do you think you need psychiatric help?"

"Yes, if I was crazy, but I am not crazy."

"Would you like to see if you really are crazy or not?"

"Sure."

"Okay, well first we're gonna take away everything, and then every person that you love. Then we're gonna have you make all kinds of legal decisions and judgments on your future status as a member of society. Then we are going to have you go back to work in four days and continue your life as if you didn't experience all these tragedies."

"Excuse me!"

"Please, Robert, don't interrupt. Then you can go to grief meetings and some grief counselling pseudo-psychiatrist, and maybe some church services, and read all you can about loss and grief. Then we can see just exactly how you have adjusted to life as you know it and how we know it. How does that sound, Mr. Piombino, I mean Mr. Robert, sorry, we mean Robert, just plain ole Robert, no Mister, no

Mr. Piombino. How does that all sound, Ron, uhhh, Rob? It is Mr. Piombino, right? We do have so many clients it gets confusing."

"No it is PIOMBINO, but that's fine, I really don't feel as if he even exists anymore. But as I was trying to say, isn't there some more accurate means of testing to see if I am crazy or normal, then just how I walk down the street and whether or not I engage in social intercourse, or if I still brush my teeth or not? Not to draw too fine a point on things, but most of the people I come in contact with I think are, for lack of a better term, and not having any medical degree myself … a lot more crazy than I am."

"Well, to be quite honest, Bob, may we call you Bob, there really isn't any proven methodology yet to prove or disprove brain damage, or mental capacity from loss of loved ones. Quite the opposite is true as we have seen many heartbroken people go on to live a splendid existence, and they get on with their lives and remarry and even start new careers and families."

"Well, that all seems fine and dandy for those lucky individuals, but what about those that feel as if their world has stopped, their light has dimmed, and they are literally alone without the person they chose to live out their days with? Is there any way to determine sanity or craziness with them, us, me? I think not, and if I act at all normal, whatever that is, it's a giant step toward some semblance of what life was like before the tragedy and tragedy and tragedy happened."

"Well, Bobby, If I may call you that, we seem to be in agreement on some many levels in so many ways, that the determination of your sanity or lack of it seems inconsequential and irrelevant, and our advice to you, Tim, is to stay the course and hang on tight because it really can't get much worse … ya think?"

Please note. This is not a verbatim copy of today's meeting with the psychoanalyst at the Poughkeepsie Institute for the Hard Headed, or soon to be.

UPDATE and additional footage: I've always felt that the best place to begin anything was the beginning, except of course when looking for something that you've lost. In that case, the end is probably your best choice, as the last place you look will be where it's found. The very beginning will never be known to me, as I was much too young to remember such important times as my initial entrance into the living, breathing place we get to inhabit for a brief while. But I do have a vivid recollection of Bob's first day in school.

KINDERGARTEN: A Dickensian Nightmare

Let's begin by placing our pencils down and sitting up straight in our chairs. The block that I grew up on had a school a few houses down from where I lived, and for the first four years of my life, I would play outside the brownstone structure, with three huge oak trees standing guard in the front courtyard. I played there with my friends on the block and always wondered what it was like inside, where all the children would go in the daytime. Bells would ring and everyone would disappear inside, sometimes never to be seen again. It was, from my young perspective, very intimidating, even though I didn't know what these words meant at the time.

Eventually when I was four and a half years old, my parents said I would be going to this building by myself to start my learning, and that I would enjoy being with so many more children close to my age. My birthday being in December at the end of the year, this meant I started school before I was five, when others were five for the whole year. I was basically the "runt." I was not too agreeable with actually going inside the big brown building as it was old and scary, and I had heard some pretty awful things being said about it by the neighborhood kids who had actually been inside this large brown monolith. I begged my parents not to make me go, and I didn't want to leave my house and my family. After all I was only four and one half years old, only recently able to skip the diapers.

When the day came, I was traumatized and gave everyone a hard time about wanting to get rid of me like this. I cried and cried all the way to the school, where I was left facing twenty-something kids my age or actually some a full year older. I was just a baby compared to the older students, and I wanted nothing at all to do with this school stuff. I was told it's only kindergarten, like that was supposed to ease my apprehensions and all would be fine. I was told about recess and nap time and it would be lots of fun and we would all make new friends and what a wonderful place it really was.

Oh boy, wow, that was some line they fed me, because I finally stopped crying and made my way into the school. I was led into Mrs. Genari's kindergarten class. There's that strange word again. Every other school grade has numbers, but this class is so special and so different that they had to give it a name instead of a number, like it was going to be different than the rest. No mere number was going to be able to identify this class, and besides, they couldn't use negative numbers as we haven't even learned positive integers yet. For sure this was going to be something quite special.

I don't recall the actual exact moment that I started to cry, but I would bet it was the very first second my mother left me alone with the teacher. Is that a correct time reference? "The first second" makes me think of numbers again, but I was now fully ensconced in this new world. A new world of chalk and blackboards and letters and numbers and wooden desks, and I just wanted to go home. I don't like this place at all. I wanted to quit school the first time I walked into the building.

Living so close to the school had hardened me to what to expect in a way, because I would play in my backyard with my toy soldiers and my friends. Just a hundred feet away was the schoolyard with bells and children running around, laughing and making noise, when teachers shouting instructions would silence the crowd. I would watch the kid's line up, like mechanical robots, in neat rows and march in separate formations back into the building. Meanwhile, I would continue playing, just a mere distraction, and they couldn't control me. I was in my backyard.

I believe Mrs. Genari's first words out of her crooked thin lips were, "Stop your crying, baby boy, or I'll really give you something to cry about." That strategy had little positive motivation or impact, and I merely continued to cry. The other children seemed to have found something to amuse each other during my indoctrination to the Huber Street School System as they were all laughing out loud as I continued to become immersed in this new reality.

No, no, it's not nap time yet. Thoroughly convinced that I had correctly anticipated my dark fate in this horrid place, I cried. I cried because I wanted to go home. I cried because I was scared. I cried for so many reasons but mainly because I was just four years old. Isn't that an acceptable thing to do at that age? Apparently, not to Mrs. Genari. She shook me about for a while and repeatedly yelled at me to "stop crying, what are you, a baby?" not wanting to hear my reply. I guess she never heard me say "Yes, that's right." So why am I being yelled at and shaken about like this? I'm not from a home where child abuse is condoned or practiced, so why is she hurting me?

The back of the classroom was basically a closet with sliding doors, and that's where this gray-haired hag was taking me, crying all the way, with other children laughing or covering their mouths because they were not completely comfortable with my mistreatment, but it was an amusing sight to see this little boy crying and being dragged to the back of the room. Kids will laugh at all kinds of things that not necessarily are actually humorous. Kids can be cruel, but teachers can be crueler.

Before I could get my balance this five-foot-tall creature had thrown me into the closet, in the dark. Alone, scared, and wet from crying, I was forced into isolation for the first time in my short life. I was now at four and a half years old contemplating my future, and the outlook was bleak indeed. I never was too fond of the dark and always slept with the bedroom door ajar to have some type of connection with the rest of the world, but this was total and complete isolation.

I wondered what I had done that was wrong and deserving of such harsh penalty. I would have stopped crying if I could, but the tears kept flowing and my little heart was racing. Fear was my only companion inside that darkened room. What a way to start my scholastic career. I had never even been in a classroom before, especially inside a closet. But there I was alone, wet, crying, scared, in absolute total fear, no family, no friends, just me inside the closet and my jailer on the other side taunting me and ridiculing me in front of other children that would remain with me through grammar school. Talk about a learning disability.

There were strange smells and textures against my tiny body that added to my discomforts and fears. I had no way of knowing why I was here, and was this how I was going to go through school … in a closet? How could I ever survive going through this every day, and this was just the first day of school. I would have cursed, but I don't think I knew any curse words back then, but I sure made up for it later in life, by adding to my vocabulary, verbose, and colorful adjectives of a mature nature used at the drop of a hat. And now back to our story …

Suddenly a blinding light from the door sliding open, breaking the darkness of my prison, and a wet substance thrown in my face, and then just as quickly the door slams shut. Back into the darkness, back into silence, only now much wetter and traumatized to the point of hysteria. But not before my tormentor, my teacher, a wicked creature yelled "maybe this will shut you up cry baby." She was wrong I cried more than before, trying to wipe whatever she had just thrown in my face.

What possible justification can there be for such horrendous abuse. I wondered what horrible crime I had committed to cause this punishment. I know I yelled at my mother recently for not letting me stay out after supper. Once I took a toy from my sister and wouldn't let her have it, and I believe I made her cry. That must be it, sure that's the reason. No, I didn't mean to make her cry, and I was sorry for getting upset at my mother, and I said out loud these thoughts so I could be forgiven and let out. After all we were Catholic.

So here I was at the tender young age of four and a half, locked in a closet of a building that I knew I didn't want to go in, forced to go there by my parents, locked in a closet by the teacher, and soaking wet from tears and the water thrown in my face. I suppose some present-day psychoanalyst or psychiatrist would find plenty of material there to explain why certain actions occurred during my life and assign blame and causation for a myriad of character flaws. But I won't because as a dear old friend of mine said when I told her this story, "It toughened you up."

Oh, if you're still there, I forgot to finish the story. After several episodes of this crazed person's indifference to a child she was supposed to protect, after repeated drenching and berating, I guess I ran out of tears, bone-dry. I was eventually released from my prison and let into the class as if nothing happened. Then standing there in front of my laughing peers, I was sent home to get dry clothes. I wish I could add something like I returned back to school and had a fine experience with the teacher and the students and all's well that ends well, but I can't. It didn't.

School Daze

I was trying not to sound like the crybaby that I was in kindergarten, but my sound reasoning has been outvoted by my other sound reasoning, and I will add a bit more about my early days in the school system. I can only assume that most people had a very nice time in grammar school and don't really have too many memories from day to day of those days. Wow, I would sure like to know what that feels like, but I stray yet again from the story.

After surviving somehow through my first year with Ms. Genari, I was promoted to the first grade. Much to my horror and chagrin, when I entered the class, who do you suppose was going to be my brand-new teacher for the first grade? It was her, as my teacher again, yes … the same woman again, another year, of a teacher who must have placed me at the bottom of her list of children she would help or be kind to or show respect toward. I was just drained of any hope of my classmates forgetting about my close encounter with the kindergarten closet on my first day of school. My heart fell to the floor as did my body a year earlier to the closet floor, but this time no tears. Apparently I had advanced or retreated into my safe place, my shell, my oasis amongst mine enemies.

I have very little if any memories of any happiness during that class. I remember liking the singing and the piano, but any actual social intercourse with my classmates is not even a distant memory to me. I have always thought how wonderful the human brain or mind is that it has the uncanny ability to completely vacate and wipe out any harmful thoughts from our consciousness. A survival mechanism, that without which I would probably have wound up in prison for multiple murders (maybe a slight exaggeration, but it sounds good for our saga).

I don't recall any further negative hair-raising, spine-chilling incidents happening in my first grade year except for one. During the morning roll call, I was too terrified to speak or answer "here" as my name was called out. I remember concentrating and trying so hard just to answer when my name was called, but the majority of times just some squeaking little inaudible sound was emitted from my throat, which usually had two effects.

The first was the children laughing at me, not understanding how hard it was for me to sit there and act like the others did, who were accustomed to being praised and coddled and gently caressed by teacher. I was scorned with total apathy toward any positive thing I did. The other effect from my inability to perform like the others was the teacher would sarcastically ask me, "What's the matter, don't you know your name?" I don't know if this happened every single day or only a few, but as I stated earlier, the brain's ability to wipe this crap off the plate so you can get on with your life is priceless. No doubt prisoners and those being tortured have to rely on this to place themselves mentally in another time and place.

I don't know where that little boy went, but I know he wasn't there for all those injustices. Some fantasy creation saved me but definitely destroyed any ability to learn or comprehend at that place. The bad thing is that while writing this story I have found tidbits of memory, partial snippets from those days that survived the cleansing, healing process of data deleting from my internal hard drive (no humor at all there, just an appropriate analogy).

I can recall crawling under some bridge-type structure built by my classmates, but as I went underneath, someone knocked it down on me, and everybody laughed and asked if I was going to cry again. This particular event is very vivid, and I can hear the voices, see and smell, the wooden boxes, and feel them hitting me. I was shocked and surprised at first, but after hearing the laughing, I realized it was just the little bastards being bastards (don't know if that's nice, but I'm leaving it in anyway, it's my story).

It was also around this time that my very best friend from "up the block" moved. He went to Catholic school and didn't know much about my trouble in my school. I was just glad to have a best friend. We ate in each other's house, and our parents were friends also. When he moved away, it was like a blanket of darkness fell over me. No sanctuary, no friendly place to go besides inward was left. I would retreat deeper into whatever place I could go to escape that school.

I had another friend "up the block," but he used to collect dead things that he found and bury them under his porch. I wonder if he wound up in jail for some wickedness and some debauchery or something. I eventually stopped being friends with him because even with my desperation I knew there may have been some tools missing from that boy's shed.

There was a Ms. Costanzia that used to come around to evaluate kids, and they even had a nut class where troublemakers and those unable to learn or acted up, disturbing others, went to. She looked like she just came out of the jungle, and modern psychiatry was still decades away when this creation was diagnosing us. What a laugh. I always wondered why they wouldn't just put me in there and be done with it, but I guess I eked out the year and eventually went to the second grade.

I knew or thought I was reasonably sure, as much as a six-year-old boy could be that I had escaped the evil confines of the wicked witch. I watched *The Wizard of Oz* for the first time and got chills down my spine whenever the wicked witch showed up. She didn't look or sound like my witch (teacher), but you couldn't convince me the movie wasn't written about her, at least the wicked witch part. I remember screaming with joy as she melted to the ground, how joyous a sight for this little frustrated, abused child.

This would be the point that in most stories is referred to as the end. Nope, no, sir, not yet, I don't think so, because this magnificent example of educational dedication and service, this teacher who dedicated her life to help others (sans myself obviously), had been rewarded for such fine service to our community and to the education of our most precious resource, our children. She was asked to accept and did accept the position of principal of Huber St. School.

And some may wonder why, I anger often, scream frequently, and use profanity at every chance. Why do I have such low expectations in life? Why didn't I graduate high school? Why do I resist closeness with others? Why do I have low self-esteem? How come I became an alcoholic? Why do I enjoy horror movies? How come I like to eat? Why do I sleep on my side? How come I squeeze pimples? Why is my favorite color blue? How come I wear a size 14 EEEE shoe? Why do I have a snake phobia? How come I like to wear women's clothing?

Well, for sure I don't have "all" these things, especially the woman's clothing bit, but it makes for fine sophisticated entertainment. In addition, they're all perfectly valid questions, easily transferred to some other story or place or person. Thanks for reading up to here, and please, turn out the lights when you leave.

A Grand Entrance Indeed

For those of you that missed the previous chapters of my "Tale of Woe" I can only offer you a brief synopsis to bring you up to speed for the following entry (boy goes to school, school sucks, and boy hates school). I must say, though, you did miss a fine rendition of an otherwise frightful experience during my first two years in the Secaucus School System.

The experiences thus described are traumatic enough that anyone needing subject matter for their psychiatric doctoral thesis would be blessed with the harvesting potential of my plight, including its eventual outcome. I have survived the experience without prejudice or malice toward any living being and have become a fully functioning, well-adapted, superbly adjusted member of modern-day society, especially on the days I'm let out to explore the grounds.

Now that all the preliminaries are cleared up, let's begin tonight's episode.

It was a fine sunny day in the small country-like village of Secaucus when this fine young boy smartly walked the few hundred yards to the Huber Street School. I walked down the hall, entered my third-grade class, with scant a memory of those tragic early years of my incarceration in the public school system (see previous chapters).

Without paying attention to details, I didn't think much needed to be thought about. I entered the class and grabbed the edge of the large oak door and pulled it shut. Unfortunately, I had removed all but two of my fingers from the path of the solid heavy oak door, and it slammed almost closed (fingers prevented actual closing) crushing and nearly severing my distal and mid phalanges (top two sections) of my middle and index digits (fingers).

Soaring pain raced through my hand through nerves and synaptic connections through my spinal cord to my thalamus and finally to the frontal cortex of my brain. Pure, unadulterated grown-up style excruciating pain had filled the life of this seven-year-old person. Pain, heat, and red filled my vision and my head. I acted from some primitive instinct left over from caveman time. From deep inside my brain, some ability allowed me to quickly race to my desk and thrust my hand inside.

I felt safe.

Not a sound or utterance articulated from my voice. No cry-baby this time. Not even a tear traced the pain down the face of this little boy, no way. Instantaneous, as the flash of pain soared through my young flesh, simultaneously the memory of the first day of school locked in that closet along with the fear and loneliness of that imprisonment filled my uncluttered mind.

In mind-numbing fear I sat there oblivious to the pain. It had vanquished along with any hope of normalcy this day. My God, what was I to do? There was blood spurting out inside my desk, and blood was everywhere, on the floor, and all over my clothes. I sat in silence and pretended to be interested in the teacher's preparation of the day's lessons as she drew in the front of the room on the blackboard.

Terror gripped me inside as I thought what would they do to me now, after all I had only cried, and they locked me in the closet, throwing water repeatedly in my face, and scolded me again and again until they broke my young spirit. All that was done just for getting some tears on their floor. What would be my punishment for getting blood everywhere? The consequences were unimaginable to me.

My fear of reprisal and my fear of uncertainty as to what would happen next was short-lived, as one little girl started screaming at the top of her lungs because she saw blood by the door. I now started to sweat profusely and recited every prayer I ever heard and quickly made up new ones in the hope that my dear Lord would take me from here and end the life of this wretched sinner. Only seven years old and I surely wanted no more from this school, and whatever it was they would do to me this time.

The teacher had calmed the little girl down and was asking if anybody was cut hurt or bleeding. As the children all looked around at each other in silence, I too silently looked around at everyone somehow hoping that someone would be found that was bleeding and that it wasn't me.

I sat in silence as the teacher started to follow the trail of blood. I wondered if it would maybe lead to a dead end. As the teacher kept calling out who's bleeding, and as she got closer to my desk, I thought I would faint or maybe have a heart attack. Then before I knew it she was there.

Standing right in front of me she asked me if I was bleeding. I shook my head and said no. She asked a little firmer. I still replied with a head shake and said no. Now she demanded to see my hand. I told her it was fine. Blood all around me with a trail of blood right to my desk, I bold-faced lied my ass off to this teacher and told her no I was not bleeding.

I knew I was caught, and this time when asked to see my hand, I pulled it out, and all the children that had surrounded my desk gave a collected sigh and gasp and screamed as they saw the fingers dangling off my hand. The teacher also covered her mouth and gasped and said something like "Oh My God."

Upon my capture, when I removed my hand from the desk, I finally felt the pain and let loose with a river of tears. Nearly unable to breathe from all the release of my pain and withheld suffering, I was able to squeak out a sentence. It was something like "Please don't punish me. I didn't do it on purpose."

I remain to this day physically and emotionally scarred by the events of that long-ago day, and I offer it as an escape for those whose simple ordinary childhoods were without horrendous, cruel, and unusual circumstance. I don't seek pity for the events of those early years. I merely write about them as a form of catharsis, a purging of evil events, and it provides me with an opportunity to practice my typing skills.

ABOUT THE AUTHOR

The author has retired from an active work life and now resides at home with his dog, his pipe, and his slippers. Observing life and reminiscing from this safe vantage point, future works are already in progress. With a mixture of unrestrained subtlety and sarcasm, the pages fill quickly with a healthy splattering of humorous anecdotes about everyday events common to all. Uncommonly brought to our attention with a fresh reality and a vivid imagination, frequently requiring rereading to ensure we get the fullness and detail that permeate most of his writings. Mr. Piombino is a lifelong resident of New Jersey and reassures his readers that no amount of money or fame would ever get him to leave his beloved place of birth.

CPSIA information can be obtained
at www.ICGtesting.com
Printed in the USA
LVHW08s0727180718
583906LV00002BA/177/P